Legends of Goodland

Interviews with Kappy Kirk
& her friends

Authored by
Elizabeth McDonald Perdichizzi

Graphics and Layout: Bill Perdichizzi

Reviewed by my friends: Marion Nicolay, Faye Brown,
& Mary Lou Jankowski

FIRST EDITION, FIRST PRINTING 2021
© 2021
All rights reserved

Library of Congress Control Number: 2021917617
ISBN 978-0-9677281-1-7

Caxambas Publishing
1200 Butterfly Court
Marco Island, Florida 34145
(239) 394 6917
Email: betsyperd@comcast.net
Web site: http://www.caxambaspublishing.com/

Introduction
Katherine "Kappy" Stephens Kirk
(1917 – 2010)

All of Kappy Kirk's life was spent on the island where she lived making her a unique individual given the mobility of the age we live in.

She combined the history of the three communities in her own person: Goodland, Marco and Caxambas.

The places she called home were the historic buildings of the island: the Marco Lodge in Old Marco (now in Goodland), the Heights Hotel, the Barfield House, both in Caxambas, and her own home in Goodland going on 100 years-old, give or take a few years. Some of the homes are still here and some have already passed into legend.

Kappy's story is a tapestry whose threads are the many people of Goodland, Marco, and Caxambas, past and present, woven through and intertwining.

In June of 1993, unaware of the singular thread that drew me to her and would lead me into writing and publishing historical books about Aunt Tommie and island history, I went to Goodland to meet her.

TABLE OF CONTENTS

INTRODUCTION 3

CHAPTER 1 7
   Meeting Kappy Kirk 7

CHAPTER 2 27
   Goodland Point 27

CHAPTER 3 36
   Betsy Meets One Of The Old Timers................................... 36

CHAPTER 4 51
   Caxambas 51

CHAPTER 5 60
   The Movie... 60

CHAPTER 6 79
   Deaconess Bedell (1875 -1969)... 79

CHAPTER 7 90
   William And Marie Ludlow 90

CHAPTER 8 102
   Marie Maps Out Goodland 102

CHAPTER 9 112
   The Hermit In Bud Kirk's Back Yard 112

"Kappy" Kirk

CHAPTER 1
Meeting Kappy Kirk

Kappy in her enclosed porch

I knocked on Kappy Kirk's door at 200 Harbor Place, Goodland, Florida one day during the rainy season. The mosquitoes were fierce that day as I dashed from the car to her side porch.

Kappy's house sits in the heart of Goodland opposite Little Bar and Stan's. I took the chance that she would be home and stopped by unannounced. I had been told that her husband Bud was the one with all the answers about the island, but he had passed and she still lived in Goodland.

"Come in this house!" she cried as she opened the screen door to let me in. "You don't have to knock, just come on in," she said.

I scurried in trying not to bring too many mosquitoes in with me as the door screen door closed behind me. Brushing myself down I introduced myself and explained why I had come, mainly to get the oral histories of the old timers before they were lost.

Kappy smiled and invited me to sit down at her kitchen table and have a cup of coffee while we talked.

I looked around at the great room/kitchen area where I sat. The living area to my left on the far wall had a grey-stone fireplace that Bud had built. Today it was filled with rows of candles in the off season and dominated one end of the room opposite a comfortable sofa and padded chairs tossed with bright throw pillows. There was a doorway near the fireplace that led to the enclosed front porch that was a combined family room and artist studio. I could just glimpse her easel, paints and brushes behind the sofa that divided the room. Kappy had become an artist in her senior years and her walls were hung with lovely paintings of tropical flowers and saltwater birds that she planned to give her grandchildren.

The kitchen end of the great room had wooden cabinet doors rising to the ceiling inlaid with clear glass to display her crockery. The sink, range and refrigerator were tucked in beneath making the combined living space roomy and inviting.

I discovered that the coffee was always on at Kappy's house and many people stopped by and were always welcomed.

I learned that the chair I was sitting in might have had have held local fishermen with their rubber boots, famous movie stars such as Christopher Plummer or Burl Ives, well known authors as Bud Shulberg the author of the *Wind Across the Everglades*, or the anthropologist Dr Henry Field curator of the Fields Museum in Chicago. It might once have held a Russian prince!

Over steaming cups of black coffee we got acquainted. Kappy moved about her kitchen pouring coffee and serving cookies, arranging fresh flowers on the table as we talked. She was a tall spare woman, straight as an arrow, with a slight limp because of a bad hip. Her face was framed by a halo of fluffy white hair setting off her direct blue eyes that crinkled when she laughed.

We talked all afternoon and I learned that afternoon to my surprise that Bud may have had the answers to my questions but it was Kappy who was the native islander, born here, and raised by her Aunt Tommie, the Queen of Marco Island. Kappy lived in both villages Marco and Caxambas. In the summer of 1949 she helped the sons of Barron Gift

Collier create the fishing village of Goodland Point, the name soon shortened to Goodland.

"Is it true that Goodland grew overnight like a mushroom?"

"Almost," she laughed, "It didn't quite grow overnight - it took a few months one hot summer."

"What happened?"

"Well, all of the fishermen from Caxambas moved overland to Goodland with their seventeen or eighteen houses."

"They brought their houses with them?"

"Yes, Harry Pettit was the only one living here before then. His house is just over there," she said pointing to the south of her.

How did he feel about everybody moving in?"

"Oh, I think he liked the company."

"Is that how you came?"

"Yes, our house was the last house to be moved. We kept the store where I worked in Caxambas till the last so people could get their groceries and mail. Then we moved it too several months later. I lived in Goodland and kept going back to Caxambas to work for a long time. I missed Caxambas it was my home. Bud missed it too."

"You weren't happy about the move?"

"It was a bad time in my life."

"Why did you move?"

"That is quite a long story let's save that for when you come again."

Kappy and I met frequently over the summer and into the fall talking about her Aunt Tommie Barfield and the people who lived in each of the villages. She had a good memory but at 77 the detail was spotty. I found full accounts of her stories in the old Collier County newspapers on microfiche at the Naples library, and in 1999 I published her aunt's story *A Girl Called Tommie, Queen of Marco*. Kappy and I began selling autographed copies of the book at Stan's restaurant across the street from her house. He was a long time neighbor of her and let us set up our card table of books for the crowd who came on Sundays to enjoy the outdoor music and dancing, and listen to his crass jokes. Every once in a while he would make an announcement and steer people our way to buy his neighbor Kappy's book.

Stan Gober, painting by Stephen Muldoon

A local legend looks back

By Marion Nicolay, columnist for the Marco Island Eagle

In the mid-seventies Stan's Idle Hour restaurant in Goodland had a weekly special of all-you-can-eat stone crab claws. It drew a great crowd with shells all over the floor and waitresses trying to keep the claws coming.

Owner Stan Gober grew up in Alabama and left high school to join the Navy in World War II. Although he earned his GED, he never used his GI Bill to attend college, something he still regrets. He has always counseled his own three sons and daughter (and later his grandchildren) to get the education he never had.

After the war, Stan worked for the phone company in Alabama for several years, finally relocating to Miami in 1954. It was then that he discovered Goodland for fishing weekends. After 15 years of coming here as often as he could, he went into debt to purchase the Idle Hour motel and later the restaurant across the street when it came up for sale. He had to sell his house and quit his job, and his wife Faye nearly went into a state of collapse at the idea of living with "all those redneck fishermen." She changed her mind when she got to know the people there. Nobody ever worked harder than Stan in those early years. While expanding the business, he once had five mortgages at one time. A friend in Michigan helped him out, and Stan never missed a payment.

"I could never have made it without the help of the Lord," he says now. A deeply religious man, he often quotes scripture while talking of his past life, and frequently says that only the help of God brought him to the point where he is today.

He and Faye raised four children including three boys: Russ is now a fishing guide, Jay and his wife moved to North Carolina where they are about to open a restaurant, and Steve, the youngest, manages Stan's Idle Hour very successfully.

"Experimenting with dope was a popular thing while the boys were growing up," Stan recalls, "I told them that it would kill them if they got involved in it, and I also said they'd never get any help from me if they got into trouble." The lesson seemed to impress them, and there was never any trouble in the Gober home.

The restaurant has grown and prospered through the years. You can go by car or boat, and Sundays are special with live music and entertainment. Dinners are not served that night because Stan feels he makes plenty of profit in the afternoons and prefers to let other local restaurants have the evening business.

When Stan's wife Fay died in 1983, he decided to stage a few benefits for cancer research. With the help of golfer Ken Venturi and Anna Yamanis, owner of the Island Woman Boutique next to the Idle Hour, he raised a great deal of money for the cause.

As he talks about his musical career, he remembers beginning with a 15-minute show which he MC'd while in the Navy, but he gives all the credit to God.

"I can't write music," he confesses, "songs come into my head and I put them down on paper and eventually make a recording, but I don't really write them."

His best-known release is a toe-tapping number called "What Kind of Fish is That?" which never fails to bring laughs and applause from a crowd, even from the tourists who are being teased in the lyrics. He made his first musical tape in 1983, and sings weekly at the restaurant.

Another inspiration came to him one day in 1985 and he staged the first Mullet Festival. This is now an annual event which attracts people from all over Florida, complete with contest for the Mullet Queen and a dance competition called the Buzzard Lope taken from one of his songs.

The Buzzard Lope
Going down the highway feeling fine
Doing 55 and right on time
Look up ahead and saw something in the
Highway, looks dead
A bunch of buzzards standing around
They all step back, with a lot of hope
Start doing the Buzzard Lope…
Flap your wings up and down
Take a few steps back
Go 'round and round

Kappy says that Stan has supported many good causes besides Cancer, the Wishing Well, and the Veterans. "The good lord put me here, I just can't say no if someone needs help," he said to County Commissioner Donna Fiala at a benefit for Kiwanis.

I remember that he hosted fund raising event when the Historical Society was trying to raise money to build a museum a museum on Marco Island.

Stan Gober, Shirley Beckwith, museum fund raiser 2005

Marion Nicolay, Virginia Carlin and Patty Marzulla

Bill and Betsy Perdichizzi, 2005

The Historical Society's professional consultant Sally Woliver, being new on the scene, was invited to attend. Sally enjoyed the whole atmosphere saying, "This was the first time she had been to a fund raising event at a rock concert!" We eventually raised enough money to build the Marco Island Historical Museum. It opened in 2010.

Stanley R. Gober died June 18, 2012 at the age of 86: father of four with 11 grand children. His celebration of life was held at the restaurant with Buzzard Lope Queen Mary, a 71 plus year old favorite, by his coffin and hundreds of people paying respects. His grandchildren carried his coffin from the restaurant. His son Steve Gober carries on the tradition his father started.

Young Kappy

    Kappy was just three and a half or four years old when she went to live with Aunt Tommie to be raised like a daughter along with Elsie 13, Elva 12, and Ava Elizabeth 10. They treated her like a baby sister.

    Kappy said she followed her aunt everywhere. They called her "Aunt Tommie's shadow" going from the Heights Hotel where they lived to the Mercantile Store on the wharf, the school house, and back again. Aunt Tommie did everything that needed to be done on the island with Kappy at her side sometimes she held school in her kitchen or in other locations. She dismissed school after a storm to pick up fish washed up on the beach to sell at the market and prevent waste; she gathered mangoes that needed gathering; or tomatoes that needed harvesting after salt water killed the vines. Another time she rescued Chinese immigrants from the beach, nothing was too big or too small for Aunt Tommie's attention.

Us Kids Swimming in Caxambas, Aunt Tommie & Juana

Schooling was important to Aunt Tommie for her children, nieces, nephews and neighbors since she had never been able to go back to school after the third grade. She began attending Lee County meetings in Fort Myers asking for schools, roads, and ferries for Marco Island. Lee County provided a school when seven children could be gotten together, so schools moved around from a shack Pig Key in Barfield Bay, to various places in Marco or Caxambas.

In 1912 she lobbied and won permission to build a shell road on the island using her father's truck. Aunt Tommie worked hard to get county officials to spend money or do anything outside of Fort Myers city limits. In 1923 she supported Barron Gift Collier's effort to carve out a new county from Lee just because she believed that he would bring the infrastructure, power lines, and paved roads to the island. Collier won the day and in return appointed Tommie Barfield Superintendent of Public Education despite her third grade schooling.

Barfield House

One day while we were talking, Kappy told me about the move from the Heights[1] hotel down to the village of Caxambas.

"Aunt Tommie and Uncle Jim sold the hotel up on the hill to Barron Collier in the 1930's and rented a company-owned house from him in Caxambas village. The teachers we had been boarding went with us to the Barfield House. It was a large two story house built by Captain Jack Collier who had moved to Fort Myers. There was a living room, dining room, small music room, kitchen, two pantries, plus three bedrooms and two baths downstairs, and four bedrooms and two baths upstairs. The family occupied the downstairs bedroom, Uncle Jim and Aunt Tommie in the middle room opposite the stairway, Elsie in the front bedroom and Kappy and Elva in the back bedroom. The upstairs rooms were rented to teachers at the school and to the Post Master Miss Jane Burdock, a girl in her early twenties who served Caxambas and Marco which included meeting the Atlantic Coastal train that came onto the island each weekday and picking up the mail. Aunt Tommie's cook Mr. Freeman lived in one of the cottages behind the Barfield House and the other cottage was occupied by Carl Salo, the handyman.

---

[1] Heights: Present day Indian Hill

"We girls liked living in the village instead of up on the Heights," Kappy said. "It was closer to Grandmother Stephen's boarding house, our friends, various cousins, the clam factory, the mercantile store and the post office. Best of all, we liked being near the water where we could go swimming in the Gulf on hot days."

Kappy's grandparents, Allen Thomas and Annie Stephens, and sister Hazel moved in the Barfield House after Elsie and Elva started high school in Fort Myers. The girls boarded with a lady in a house that Aunt Tommie rented so they could go to high school. They were only home on holidays and a few weekends. The whole family brothers, sisters, nieces, nephews all enjoyed a warm and close relationship. There were many social gatherings around the piano or the Victrola when the girls played records and danced.

Scripps School (Aunt Tommie center back)

Aunt Tommie, as Superintendent, helped hire teachers for the new Scripps School that opened in 1927 and she also boarded some of them. It was the first consolidated school on the island named for the family who bought the old Ludlow place and donated land for the new school. In 1936 a new teacher was hired for the school, Mr. Frank Heath. He and his wife Thelma and their two year old son Frankie moved into one of the upstairs rooms at the Barfield House. Frank was appointed Principal.

"We didn't like the arrangements because sand fleas came in the screens at night and bit little Frankie," wrote Thelma in her memoir. "However, it was the only place for us to live, no other house was available. We agreed to stay one week and we ended up staying for the next ten years."

There were three teachers at Scripps School: Miss Parker nearly 70 years old taught grades one two and three, Ruby Rollins in her 50's taught grades four, five and six, and Frank taught grades seven through twelve.

When a huge carbuncle developed on Frank's spine he couldn't teach, Aunt Tommie asked his wife Thelma to take the classes even though she didn't have a teaching certificate. She said she would if Uncle Jim agreed to keep little Frankie along with his grandson Jimmie Dyches so Thelma could teach.

"No problem," he said.

Then Miss Parker became ill and died before the end of the year and Aunt Tommie asked Kappy to take her classes. Kappy had been living at the Marco Lodge where she helped make salads. She was happy to move back to the Barfield House in Caxambas.

Kappy and Thelma both enjoyed teaching school and took the State teacher's examination that October which allowed them to teach the following year. They began attending summer schools toward obtaining their teaching degrees.

Sometimes late at night Thelma, Jane, and Kappy rummaged in Mr. Freeman's kitchen to make candy. The old cook thoroughly disapproved of anyone using his kerosene refrigerator, his kerosene stove, and his kitchen, even though they bought the flour and sugar themselves. He put the kitchen off limits by padlocking everything including the refrigerator before he went to bed!

One night about 10:00 p.m. Kappy and Thelma became *munchy hungry*. They decided to get Jane up and go down to Mack Brawner's fish house on the wharf to get something to eat. Mack had cold soft drinks, salty crisp crackers, pickles, and the best cheese in the world. He was asleep in the little bedroom behind the store but obligingly opened up; he didn't seem to mind being awakened by the girls.

Not long after this Kappy went to visit Elva who had married Grits Griffiths and was running the G & G Mercantile store in Old Marco. Arthur Perry "Bud" Kirk came into the store while she was there and Elva introduced him. Bud was a handsome fellow with bare feet and suntanned smile. He was seven years Kappy's senior and had a touch of the homespun philosopher about him that Kappy liked. He had been on Marco about two years before catching her eye. Kappy thought he looked wonderful.

Bud came to Marco in the mid '30's and soaked up the lore of the island to the extent that most people thought he was a native of the island; going barefoot was a trademark with Bud. He lived in a little camp on Bear Point and fished off the trestle. On a good night he said he could catch 400 pounds of Snook. Fishing was his first love, his occupation and his hobby.

When he was not fishing he took odd jobs. On the day he met Kappy he was working on a Greek sponge boats tied up at the Marco dock. He said the sponge divers needed him to stay on board and protect them with a gun while they were down diving all day. He invited Kappy to go out with them one day when they went to the Everglades and she did. She was impressed that the Greek crewmen only ate once a day. Since the divers couldn't dive with anything in their stomachs no one else ate anything either, except for black olives. The evening meal when it finally came was served in one big round dish about four inches tall. The food was similar to a soufflé. The bread was so hard it had to be soaked to soften it. Then a piece was broken off and used to scoop up the food. "No dishes to wash! Kappy said. The Greek Spongers and the Bahamian conchs had a rivalry between them with Cape Romano as the dividing line. Boats caught infringing on either side had been set on fire when divers were down.

Sponges Off Loaded

As the sponge industry declined Bud picked up other odd jobs. Bud liked to explore the island and the surrounding keys. Kappy went with him sometimes.

"I never knew where we were when I went with Bud. One day we were in Goodland Point looking at the Indian Shell Mounds. We went through the brush and climbed up 16 feet to the top and down and climbed another one, and another, all 16 feet high and spaced 16 feet apart. Bud learned about birds, plants, animals and Indian artifacts by exploring and reading books."

He took a job as a game warden for the Audubon Society and was gone weeks at a time.

Kappy missed him.

After Kappy showed such an interest in the young man, Aunt Tommie helped Bud acquire a little fishing boat. She wrote a letter to his aunt who happened to be a patron of hers using the stationery she had of the Democratic Committee that just happened to be handy.

FLEM C. DANE, Chairman,   TOMMIE BARFIELD, Vice Chairman,   A. J. BERTRAM, M. D., Secretary

DEMOCRATIC EXECUTIVE COMMITTEE
OF THE
FOURTH CONGRESSIONAL DISTRICT
OF FLORIDA

Collier City, Florida
April 8, 1939

Mrs. Arthur C. Usher
Marble Head, Mass.

My dear Mrs. Usher:-

I am writing to you in the interest of Bud Kirk. He has an opportunity to get a good boat at a very great bargain. He is too modest to ask you to lend him the money but wants awfully bad to get the boat. He could make some money if he could borrow enough money to get the boat and fix it up. So I decided I would write you and give you an opportunity to help Bud help himself.

I have helped Bud get a small fishing boat but at this time of the year one cannot make anything fishing but can do well taking parties out with this size boat. I believe Bud could pay you back with interest at eight per cent, as that is Florida's interest rate. Bud has always spoken so highly of you and your ability to make money, I thought you might be willing to make him the loan. He would need three hundred dollars. If I had the money to spare I would lend it to him but I do not have it at this time and the opportunity will slip away if he cannot get the money immediately.

Bud likes to take parties out and he is thrown with a good class of people, which broadens him from the association. He also learns a great deal as he goes along so that you will really be helping him an awful lot. You could make the loan safe by taking a mortgage on the boat. I would be glad to see to that for you.

Pardon my writing to you about the interest of your own people but I have had this happen to me and I appreciated it and I believe you will too. At any rate I have done what I would like to have someone do for me under similar circumstances. I hope you had a nice trip home and that you enjoyed your stay while here. A night letter to Bud would help a lot. Kindest regards to your husband.
Sincerely,
Mrs. Tommie C. Barfield
PS: Bud does not know I am writing to you.

Aunt Tommie's letter

The loan came through and Bud bought the boat and turned to fishing for his livelihood. In the slow season he worked as manager of the Doxsee Clam Factory. He was working there when he proposed to Kappy and she accepted.

Kappy and Bud were married February 23, 1941. The ceremony was held at St. Francis Xavier Church in Fort Myers with the Reverend Father James B. Cloonan officiating. Elva was her bridesmaid and a friend from the factory was Bud's best man. The small wedding party in Fort Myers included Aunt Tommie, Uncle Jim, and Kappy's mother Josie. Aunt Tommie and Uncle Jim hosted a wedding reception at the Lodge on Marco for two hundred invited guests. Thelma crafted the wedding bell.

Our wedding

After Kappy and Bud married they lived in Marco near the Doxsee Clam factory where Bud worked.

When World War II broke out Mack Brawner, owner of the fish house in Caxambas, decided that he would volunteer for Service. When he was called for his physical he lost his nerve and drank gin the night before that elevated his blood pressure. He was told to come back in a few days. This happened a couple times but on the third time he stayed sober and ended up in the service. He was assigned to serve in the Pacific. Readers will be glad to know that he survived the war. A newspaper article in January 1949, reported by Kappy, 'Our old friend Mack Brawner, now proprietor of a retail grocery in Punta Gorda was highest bidder for the 3,400 pounds of salted mullet caught in the off season. He got them for ten cents a pound.'

Mack Brawner's Store
(The man standing on the left side of the truck is Carl Salo who lived in cabin behind the Barfield House and other Caxambas residents.)

"When Mack was finally accepted in the army he offered the little store to Bud and me," Kappy said. "We jumped at the chance because I could move back to Caxambas, and Bud could get out of the clam factory business and back to fishing, which is what he loved. We accepted right away and moved in."

"Bud would catch fish to sell at the Fish House on the wharf while I worked in the little store. We lived in the small bedroom where Mack had lived. It was good enough for a start, the price was right, and best of all we were home!

"I worked at the store during the day while Bud fished. He brought in his catch and iced it down. Sometimes after supper, he would go back out in his boat for another haul. Bud Kirk lived to fish.

"'Mack's one room wasn't actually big enough for two people. It was so primitive the tide acted as our plumbing system, if you know what I mean," she said with a smile.

"When Tom Curry's two bedroom house came open we were quick to rent it for $15.00 a month. The space seemed enormous after our one bedroom behind the store. Furthermore we could enlarge the store.

The white-framed Curry house became our real home. Tom had built the house out of salvaged heart of pine lumber that he bought from Captain Ferg hall, the lumber that was found floating in the Gulf after the 1910 Hurricane.

"I loved my new home. For the first time in my life I had a real kitchen of my own, even though I didn't know how to cook. Aunt Tommie always had Mr. Freeman do the cooking and he didn't like people messing about in his kitchen. I could set tables and make salads as I had done at the Marco Lodge, but I didn't know how to cook!

"It was like playing house. The kitchen had a kerosene refrigerator and oil stove, and a deep enamel kitchen sink with running water. I put my dishes and crockery away in the cupboard and admired how they gleamed through the glass windows in the cabinet doors.

"My cooking wasn't always successful. One evening during dinner, Bud took a bite of his canned corn, and asked, "What brand of corn did you buy? I told him the name."

He said, "Please don't buy that brand anymore, Kappy, it is much too watery."

"Aren't you supposed to add a can of water to the corn?

"Bud never let me forget that incident," she said with a twinkle in her eye.

"Our house had two bedrooms and a bath off a little hallway from the living room, dining room and kitchen on one side. The front porch was as wide as the house, and at the rear was a small screened in back porch that we turned into a bedroom when Pop Kirk or Bud's brother Damas paid us a visit."

CHAPTER 2

Goodland Point

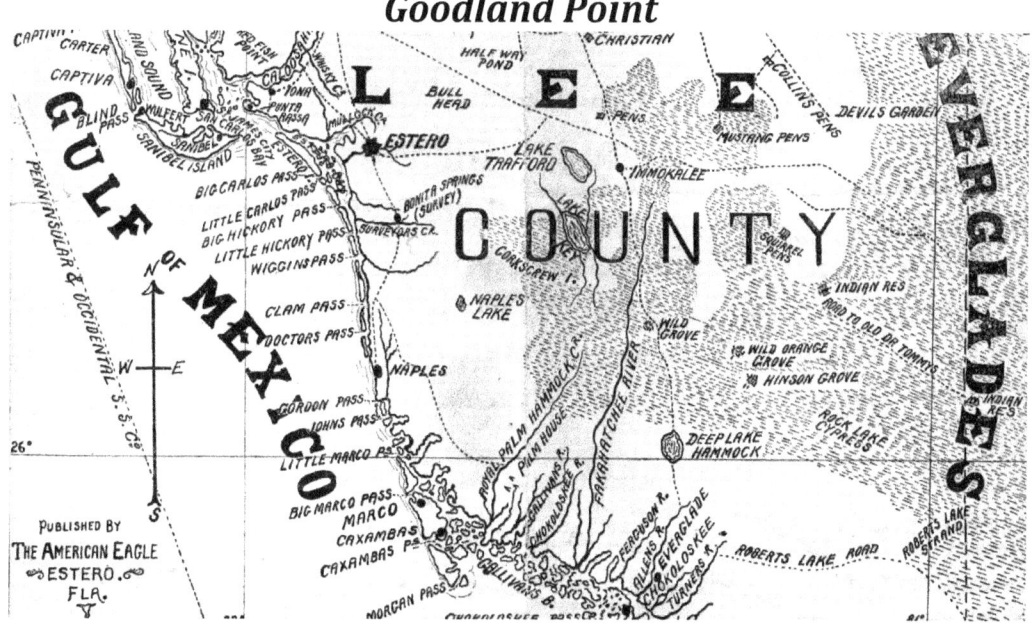

**Map from the American Eagle newspaper
Estero, Florida, 1913**

The villages of Marco and Caxambas are little black dots on this 1913 Lee County map. There is no dot for Goodland, it did not exist.

A military campaign in 1841 and 1842 recorded the first mention of an *unusual island*, which historian D. Graham Copeland thought to be Goodland Point[2] in the government's campaign against the Indians.

Johnny Roberts was the first settler and established squatter's rights. He named it *Goodland Point* for the rich black dirt. The soil was only inches deep and covered forty-acres of three 16 foot high shell mounds. The river provided a deep channel around the shell mounds leading six miles north to the Marco settlement and seven miles south to the Caxambas settlement.

Samuel Alexander Pettit bought Robert's rights in 1890. He was a farmer from Pennsylvania who migrated to northern Florida with his wife Collious Isabel Brownlow Pettit, and children and their grandmother.

The Pettits' were farming near Clearwater when the Civil War broke out. S. A. Pettit enlisted and was sent without his family to the newly activated Union Army post in Fort Myers in 1864.

---

[2] Florida's Last Frontier, Charlton Tebeau, page 42.

Fort Myers was the only federally occupied fort in peninsular Florida. It was garrisoned primarily by the 2nd Florida Cavalry, made up mostly of refugees, a recently detached company of 110th New York Infantry and 250 black soldiers of the 2nd Regiment of the United States colored Infantry, both from Fort Taylor in Key West. Fort Myers was also to be used as a refugee center for escaped slaves and Union sympathizers who were being persecuted by the secessionist who were burning their homes and driving them off their farms. At one period during the re-occupation of the Fort which had begun in January of 1864 over 400 people crowded into the fort grounds.

Confederate soldiers came to the Pettit's Clearwater farm one day begging food and threatening to take the horse and buggy. Plucky Isabel Pettit pulled a shot gun on them saying, "You are not going to take everything and leave me out here alone with no way to get out with the children." The soldiers backed down but said they would return by nightfall. She lost no time in harnessing the horse and buggy and piling her large family in and drove them to Tampa over 23 miles away. Once there she sold the horse and buggy for enough money to get her entire family on a boat to join her husband to Fort Myers.

After the war they bought the claim and settled on Goodland Point. Samuel Pettit tried farming but the shallow soil did not produce enough to make a living so he and his older sons began hunting, fishing and raising hogs and chickens to feed the family. They had to "run a panther out of the hog pens and scare off the bobcats from the chicken yard."

Samuel and Isabel raised seven children: five sons Chester, Elmer, Joseph, Marion, Harry and two daughters Clara and Carol. The older children took care of the younger down to the youngest child Harry. Samuel hired a tutor for his children the first two years and then Lee County opened a school in the vicinity.

In 1892 Lee County provided a teacher in Caxambas when seven students could be gotten together. Early schools moved around depending on student population, sometimes schools were held on Little Marco, Horr's Island, Pig's Key out in Robert's Bay, or Caxambas. The children and teachers rowed skiffs to school wherever it was held.

The older Pettit boys hunted, fished, and clammed; their sisters eventually married locals who were sea captains, clam diggers, fishermen, or fishing guides.

Burnham Clam factory, Caxambas Florida

Clamming

Pioneers had been digging clams using digging sticks at low tide in the surrounding keys since the early days. The waters teemed with quahog, hard-shell, and littleneck clams south of Marco Island. The ancient beds extended from Chokoloskee and Rabbit Key to below Harney River with the richest area extending off Coon Key about 10 miles south of Marco Island to Pavilion Key. It was said to be 20 miles long with clams as large as a man's two fists held together.

When the Burnham Clam Factory opened in Caxambas in 1904, Elmer and Joseph joined the diggers who camped out on various keys, harvesting clams and filled the skiffs waiting for the factory boats to collect them. Sometimes they worked at the factory with other men and women standing over the steam tables to clean, sort, and cook the clams

Chester found work cutting cordwood for the furnace at the Burnham Clam factory, "I rowed from Goodland Point to Caxambas every day. Many a time I would tow a lighter to one of the islands or keys that was high enough where I could cut buttonwood. I cut my way through the brush until I got to where I could cut wood. Then I cut it and hauled it on my back, one cord[3] at a time," Chester told his grandchildren.

"I would load the lighter until I got *a few cords* of lumber. Then I towed that heavy load back to Caxambas. When I reached the factory I hauled it off to the boiler which was quite a ways from the factory. The work was not easy."

---

[3] Cord: One cord of wood is 8-feet high by 4-feet wide by 4-feet deep

He found time to meet and fall in love with one of the Rojas girls who was working at the clam factory. She was one of eight Rojas girls and one brother living with their mother in one of ten cottages that Jim Barfield constructed for the factory family workers.

She and her family had been smuggled out of Cuba in 1903 by their favorite Uncle Antonio Lopez. He was an opera singer who had traveled all over and knew the ways of the world. When the large family of girls was threatened by a corrupt politician, Uncle Antonio smuggled them out to the lighthouse by Cuba. From there they caught a boat and took refuge with another uncle who lived on Chokoloskee Island near Everglades City.

Two Clam Factories on Marco Island

When the Burnham Clam Factory opened in Caxambas 1904 with ten cottages for families, it was an answer to the Rojas' prayers. The family made Caxambas their home; five of the eight girls married local men and remained in the county.

"They made the best clam chowder, so fresh and so good that it was in high demand," Chester told his grandson Elmer, "As kids we would swing by and they would give us a cup. It was canned and shipped to Key West for distribution."

In 1910, the news of the factory attracted the attention of James Harvey Doxsee whose family had been in the clam business in Ipswich, New York for generations. When the clam beds up north were depleted J. H. and his brother built a factory ship and traveled down the coast to North Carolina to harvest clams. When J. H. read in the newspapers about the success of the Burnham factory he came to Marco to see for himself. Captain Bill Collier of Marco offered Doxsee five acres of land if he would build the factory in Marco following Jim Barfield's example in Caxambas and. J. H. "Stud" Doxsee opened the Doxsee Clam factory in the Marco settlement in 1911.

J. H. Doxsee's granddaughter, Louise Thornton Anderson, remembered her grandfather, "My grandfather canned clams, and he also cooked and canned clam chowder. When he had canned his own allotment of Doxsee Clams and Doxsee Clam Chowder, he would can clam chowder for the Campbell's Soup Company. It was the same chowder, only the labels were different. I can still remember the large vats of clam chowder, and my grandfather standing on a ladder, stirring the chowder with a boat oar. The clams were then canned and it was on to the tables where the ladies pasted labels on them.

"The factory had electricity and running water, but our homes did not. The electricity for the factory was produced by a huge diesel engine. We had cisterns for water and my father, Harry Thornton, used to take the factory's dump truck and go the middle of the island where there was a fresh-water well; fill as many 55 –gallon drums as would fit in the truck, and bring them to our homes as well as to anyone else he knew needed the water. These drums sat on our back porches to supplement the water from the cisterns. In those days you did not waste water as it was a very precious commodity. Since there was no indoor plumbing, we had what was known in those days as a "house and a path;" ours was a three seater, very up scale. We cooked on kerosene stoves and lit our homes with kerosene lamps.

"During the hurricanes, we would all go to the Hotel, because it was several stories high."

Orla making clam chowder
(Courtesy of Faye Brown)

Marco Island remained without access to the mainland until 1912 when Tommie Barfield succeeded in convincing the commissioners to provide a one car ferry from the mainland to a ferry landing in the Marco Village. A few years later she lobbied successfully for a four-car, self powered ferry. Soon there were 15 cars on the island with only five miles of road, part of which was rhythmically flooded at low tide!

Harry Pettit sold most of his property to Barron Gift Collier in 1922-23 except what he kept for himself. Collier a business tycoon and land developer from New York bought up a million acres in southwest Florida including most of the Marco Island with the exception of Capitan Bill Collier's holdings in Marco.

Barron Collier had big plans to deepen the Caxambas channel to create a shipping port on the order of what Henry Flagler had done in Miami. He planned to bring in barges and steamships, to build highways and communication lines and a large hotel that would rival others on the Heights, we now call Indian Hill.

If Barron Collier controlled the county issues he could eliminate all the drawbacks to development that Tommie Barfield faced. In May of 1923 Barron Collier did two things: he instigated State Representative R. A. Henderson to sponsor a bill carving out a new county from Lee County and he asked Tommie Barfield to attend the meeting and speak about her difficulty getting tax dollars for her part of the county.

"Let the legislators decide the county division issue instead of a lengthy public referendum!" Bill # 305 before the House designated Everglade as the new county seat. Collier County (named for the pioneer family, not Barron Collier) would be made up of 57 of the 110 Lee County townships, was only two sevenths of the total valuation of Lee County. Furthermore, the Collier holdings had already paid the great bulk of taxes in southern part of Lee, and most importantly, it was pledging to finish the Tamiami Trail which had languished for lack of revenue, men and supplies.

The Bill faced massive opposition aided by the entrenched politicians who were backed by the power of the press.

Barron Collier's shrewd move to send red headed Tommie Barfield of Marco Island, whom he had met at Lee County meetings, to speak on the bill's behalf turned the tide. She had impressed him when she lobbied so successfully for schools, roads, and ferries, and Mrs. Barfield impressed the legislators when she turned a faulty telegram meant to discredit her against the county officials who sent it. She clearly demonstrated to state legislators the forces at work, the shorted-sightedness even to deceit that had forestalled any progress in the past. The Bill passed 52 - 27 against.

Governor Hardee signed the bill into law creating Collier County on July 8, 1923. Tommie Barfield was appointed the first Superintendent of Public Instruction despite her third grade education. She served her appointed term, was elected to another term, after which she resigned to take a critical position on the School Board she served for the next 20 years until her death in 1950.

Goodland Swing Bridge

After Collier County was formed in 1923, Harry Pettit went to the new county seat Everglade (now called Everglades City) asking for a road from Marco to Goodland Point; he wanted to bring his truck over to Goodland Point. The county responded they didn't have the equipment to do anything for him at the time. Not wanting to wait, Harry acquired a number of 50 gallon drums, built a platform on it and rafted his truck over himself.

When the old swing bridge from the Caloosahatchee River at Fort Myers was brought to Goodland Point to span the Marco Pass, Harry Pettit was inspired to construct a road to meet the bridge and talked to county officials about it. The agreed to black top it if he built it.

There was a shell ridge parallel with the home sites on Goodland Point that ran all the way to Royal Palm Hammock. He ringed the trees along the shell ridge and let them die exposing the ridge. Every afternoon he loaded his pickup truck with washtubs full of shell and with his wheel barrel began filling in the low spots. Soon he had a snake like roadbed that the county then blacktopped. Behold the historic curving road to Goodland!

The ancient Indian shell mounds turned out to be a natural source of revenue and building material for Harry who mined the shells to build state road 92A or San Marco Road completed in 1938. The ferry at the north end of the island was discontinued when the bridge opened.

The lagoon in Goodland Point was created when shells were taken to build Naples airport runways. Eventually houses were built around it.

Lagoon Basin

During the Florida Land Boom Barron Collier owned hotels in Useppa, Boca Grande, Punta Gorda and Everglades besides his million acres. He owned the north end of Fort Myers Beach and acquired the morning paper Fort Myers *News Press* (which had been so against him) and the evening newspaper the *Fort Myers Tropic*. Interestingly, Fort Myers remained the basis of his operation for business and newspapers, since his new county had not yet developed its own large urban city.

The Land Boom was followed by the Land Bust which was the onset of the Great Depression. It collapsed his dreams. Barron Collier died of a stroke at the beginning of the Great Depression and most of his property fell into receivership while death taxes were paid off, Collier marriages and divorces took place and new children were born for the next twenty years to complicate the issue.

CHAPTER 3

Betsy Meets one of the Old Timers

Early Caxambas

Kappy wanted me to meet her friend and a shirt-tail cousin Elmer Pettit who had grown up in Caxambas.

"We have relatives in common," she explained to me. "Elmer's father Chester and my father John Stephens both married Rojas girls."

Elmer now lived in Naples and had invited us to come see him. Kappy and I drove separately because she had errands to run in Naples. When you live on Marco Island you save up all your errands to run in the one day when crossing the Judge Jolley bridge and going to town.

I arrived at Elmer's house just before Kappy and introduced myself. Elmer was moving slowly after a recent heart attack and hadn't reached his chair when Kappy knocked. He returned to the door and greeted her at the door by saying, "Did you get lost?"

"No, "Kappy quipped, "I wasn't lost, I knew where I was; I just didn't know where you were."

Elmer's son Gary came home from work about that time to be jumped on by his pet dogs. As he tended the animals and served us ice tea; I took out my tape recorder with permission and started recording. My tape started up in the middle of their conversation about the lumber found floating in the Gulf after a storm.

Elmer turned to me and said rather pointedly, "My Aunt Rosa and Uncle Tom Curry built the house out of wood that Uncle Ferg Hall found floating in the gulf. That is the house that Kappy is now living in on Harbor Place."

Kappy immediately interjected, "Tom Curry is the one that picked up that lumber."

"No-o-o, that was Uncle Ferg Hall and it was my Dad that picked it up out in the gulf on his schooner."

"What was the name of the schooner again? Was that the Falcon?" Kappy asked.

"No, it was the Eureka. The Falcon was exactly the same as the Eureka; Captain Bill Collier built both of them exactly the same. He built one for my uncle and one for the clam factory. My uncle's was the Eureka."

Filling me in on his family relationships Elmer said, "Uncle Tom married my Aunt Concha, he used to call her Conchita. Uncle John Stephen's wife was Juana Rojas, we called her Aunt Nana. It was simple for us children. She was the one that got breast cancer."

"I remember that Aunt Tommie took her to John Hopkins," remarked Kappy.

"Yes, but she never made it. She is the one that wanted to adopt me, but my mother was furious because her sister already had four kids."

Speaking directly to Kappy again he continued his line of thought, "My Uncle John and your grandfather, old man A. T. Stephens, they both tried farming for a few years. Two or three of them branched off.

"Some rowed a boat over to Caxambas like my father Chester to work in the clam factory. I know when my father and mother married he built our house there. He built a big tank under it to hold rainwater; they always had enough fresh water. Later on that tank was destroyed and then he built an addition to the back of the house that had a cistern underneath it with a pump. The big house is not there now, there was an argument about it, but it was torn down. They should have kept that house."

I asked him if he had any pictures of it. "No my sister Connie has the old pictures of the house. The old pictures from the island my brother had all those. They rented the house to some people who took everything they had."

"I've got my memories for it all, right up here," Elmer said pointing to his head.

"When I was a kid in Caxambas, my father had to re-nail that house he built. The lumber was floating in the salt water so long that it was rusting the nails through. He had to re-nail that whole house.

"The Ludlow's house once belonged to Uncle Ferg Hall.

"I was born and raised in Caxambas, there were lots of young boys my age and the age of my brother Lawrence. We had a baseball team of just our age. Just right! There was a fellow that used to be involved in baseball and he got us organized a team. We had quite a good team all made up of Caxambas boys.

There was Thomas Albury, Richard Albury, Dan and Jim Leo, the Rawls, my brother Lawrence and I. We didn't have uniforms, just divided up sides and played each other, I was a fielder and my brother was pitcher. We had gloves and a bat. The ball field had a grocery store pretty close to the clam factory. Behind that was a big dock. It had a diving board on the dock. My brother and friends used to go down there and dive off of the dock. We used to go down and swim. It was shallow. There was a channel and it was deeper, all of younger ones would swim there."

Elmer was tiring so Kappy and I said goodbye to him. On the way out we talked a little with his son Gary who had given up his job with the Smithsonian to move back with his dogs to help his Dad. Gary also contributed to our knowledge telling us that as a boy growing up in Caxambas he had helped Mr. Ernest Otter take the busycon shells from the mound and build the retaining walls for his garden in Caxambas that is now Otter Mound Park. He remembered the Barfield House could be seen through the trees from there.

On the way home Kappy was highly amused that Elmer caller her home on Harbor Place Uncle Tom Curry's house. "I rented it, moved it, and have owned it, for 52 years!"

Goodland Point becomes Goodland Village

Goodland Village 1953

Kappy stepped quite naturally into her aunt's shoes taking care of people as Aunt Tommie began to decline. In 1948 after the death of their father, Barron Collier's three sons Barron Jr., Samuel, and Miles asked Kappy's help when it was time to develop their father's holdings on the island in Caxambas and Goodland Point.

After twenty some years it was time to develop the company-owned property in Goodland Point that was not tied up with taxes. The Collier Corporation scraped off three to four feet from the top of the large shell mounds and subdivided it into residential and commercial lots.

Collier Company Dedication Ceremony and Fish Fry

"Bud and I helped Miles Collier build a platform for the dedication. Miles spoke to the crowd. He wanted me to speak. I said, 'Miles, I don't know what to say.'"

"He said, 'Oh Kappy just get up and say the Collier Company has put the ball in your corner and you are going to run with it' or words to that effect.

"We had a big fish fry afterwards many people came from this area. Some other officials spoke. When I spoke, I said, 'I have the ball in my court and I am going to run with it.'

"I was Postmaster, but I also worked for the Collier Company, I made them a lot of money. If anything was sold, I would call Mr. Huntoon and tell him about it. At that time I had my real estate license, but I never made any money, I would just tell Mr. Huntoon about things and he would make the sale. They collected the money, I never charged them a commission or anything. If they needed some information on things, I would find out about it for them. Things that they would have asked Aunt Tommie to do fell to me. It lasted until Mr. Huntoon retired from the Collier Company."

Miles Collier asked Bud and Kappy to host a big fish fry on Sunday March 27, 1948 and issued invitations to all islanders and their guests to come. No lots would be sold on Sunday but they would have a chance to preview the site, first choice of the lots will be given to residents of the Island.

The residents of Caxambas were told, "If you buy a company lot in Goodland, with no money down, reasonable rates, and three years to pay, the Corporation will move the house you are renting free of charge, and put it on the lot you buy. You will become instant home owners in Goodland."

Miles Collier and I at the fish fry - 1948

"Most of the people coming over from Caxambas were not farmers, they were fishermen. That is how they made their living. They just needed to live in a place where they could keep their boats and have access to the water. Goodland was a good place to park their boats on the Marco River.

"It was a good deal," Kappy said, "and they knew it. People couldn't stay where they were because they didn't own the property, so most of them accepted the terms and were happy about it."

Although Aunt Tommie was aware of the move she was growing older and in declining health. She fell about this time and broke her leg and was quite incapacitated. She remained at the Lodge in Marco for a time and then was brought over to the Barfield House in Caxambas where she died in 1950.

"After the fish fry Bud told me to go over to Goodland Point and choose a lot because he was busy with something. I made my selection. I chose an oversized lot in the heart of Goodland Point. After the move we started calling our new home Goodland. I remember that the property was just white with heat that day. The contrast of the pristine white-shell and the lush green vegetation of Caxambas made me sick. I went home discouraged. We bought another piece of land down on the end for my mother Josie, but she didn't want to come over so we sold that property. We bought the piece where the fish house is a little later.

"Beginning in June of 1949, the first little wooden houses of Caxambas were loaded on a moving truck from Fort Myers and carried up the Caxambas dune ridge and out of sight to be placed down on the southeastern side of the island. It couldn't have been more foreign over there than if we had landed on the moon.

"Pat Leo's house went first, followed by White, Pettit, and Ludlow homes, then came Johnson, Bauer, and Bower in order. One by one the houses were put on a truck and trailed over the dune ridge, along the narrow finger of mangrove swamp that led to Goodland. Only scar patches remained where houses had been making it ugly in both places.

"Bud and I watched the last neighbor leave. I remember looking up at the abandoned Heights Hotel and over the trees to the Barfield House, both would be abandoned, both had been my home. Pettit's Ideal Fish Camp and a few other houses would be the only things left of Caxambas Village. It was an indescribable feeling. I looked at Bud and tried to smile."

"We're next," he said with a nod.

Kappy explained to me that her house and store were the last to be moved, "When the time finally arrived, I asked the two men who came to move the house, 'What do I do to get ready?'"

'Don't pack a thing, it is all coming with you, one said.'

'Just walk out and leave it, said the other.'

"The men knew the routine well by now, they had moved 15 or 16 houses. In preparation for the move, our house had been set up on jacks at each of the four corners. The plumbing had been disconnected and the electricity shut off. In Goodland the house would have to do without water, electricity, and plumbing for quite some time.

"The store would be the last to move, so people could get their supplies and mail. In Caxambas the store had electricity but in Goodland it would have a generator in a little shed behind the building to provide lights and keep the drink boxes cool. The generator wasn't big enough to cool both boxes at the same time, so I had to go out and switch them from time to time."

Moving my house

On my lot in Goodland

Kappy's House Move

"Early that morning Bud left to go fishing. 'Nothing for me to do here, he said as he took his fish net, gear, and disappeared before dawn. I'll see you in Goodland Point tonight.'

"I did what the movers suggested I didn't pack a thing. I made breakfast for the children. Kare was eight-years old, Tommie Dee or T.D. as we called her was two, and we had Frances Lowe, a little friend staying with us, she was thirteen or fourteen. Frances was living with us while her parents were down in the Keys fishing. Together we washed up a few dishes and put them away in the cupboard. It didn't take long to get ready to go.

T. D. and Kare

"Frances followed Kare outside when they heard the truck with the men rumble to a stop before the house. I called them back to get dressed. We were going to work at the store as usual while the house was being moved. In a very few minutes the children had their faces wiped and their clothes on. I called Frances, picked up T. D. and took Kare by the hand. I remember thinking as we stepped from the porch onto the ground that it would be the last time I stepped from the house on Caxambas soil.

"I had been born in Caxambas and my two children were born there; only the house was coming with us. I didn't want to think about it. I said to the children, 'We woke up in this house in Caxambas this morning and tonight we'll go to sleep in this house in Goodland,' as my heart sank their eyes gleamed with excitement.

"They put the house on carriers and brought it overland and set it down. It was hard to get this house off, because it was on a cement foundation underneath. They took two 2x6 boards and just propped up the porch roof when they brought it over. They just sat it on the ground. Bud had to jack it up and put in a foundation later.

"We were one of the last to come over because Bud didn't want people to say we got all the water or something like that.

"When they jacked up the store there wasn't enough support underneath and the store cracked. They had to cut it in half to bring it over."

Cash and Carry Store

The Store

"The house was moved in '49, the store was moved in '57 or '58. In 1949 I was living in Goodland and going back over to work in the store in Caxambas so people could get their mail and supplies. When they moved the store one half at a time they had to put it back together in Goodland. They didn't align it properly putting it together, so the wavy shelves of can goods made me seasick. We had to take everything off the shelves, and take the shelves and miss-align them so they looked straight with to the eye. The post office was in the store. I wasn't postmaster at the time in '49, Cora Leo was. She was also teaching school and her husband would come over, he was supposed to be postmaster, but I was doing the work. Finally, the Board of Education told her she would have to retire from one job or the other. She gave up the post office and that is when I took over in 1950.

"How did you feel about the move?" I asked.

"That was a bad time in my life," Kappy answered. "It was a terrible time…," she changed the subject.

"You think the mosquitoes are bad now; we don't have mosquitoes! I used to go out in the store walking in the afternoon because I sat in the store all the time and didn't get much exercise. So I would go home and put on long pants and a long sleeve white shirt. I would start out walking fast and the Mosquitoes would eat me up. I would run just as fast as I could run. I could look back and there would be a solid black streak of mosquitoes following me. I bet there were ten million of them. If you stopped you'd be covered. They could keep up with me too. If we didn't have sprays now we would have a lot of mosquitoes in the rainy season. If you had no rain we wouldn't have so many. But, if we had a lot of rain, so that it kept flowing, but if you had just enough rains to dampen everything down and create little puddles that would dry up in a day or so, we would have a fresh crop every morning. Then they would eat you up."

"Weren't there mosquitoes in Caxambas?"

"Oh, they had mosquitoes like that in Caxambas too. We would mix up a mixture of kerosene and oil and paint all the screens. In a short time you'd have to take them down and wash the screens and paint them all over again. There would be so many mosquitoes stuck to the oil stuff air couldn't get air through the screens. They were really bad."

"Did you ever regret the move?"

"I would NEVER have moved from Caxambas if I didn't have to, because it was home," she said with a look of pain passing over her face. "Bud liked it too because the back door was on the water. He used to say, 'Well, we could use about 200 pounds for the fish house tonight,' so he would go out and catch 200 pounds of fish, in a rowboat, by himself. That was after working at the little store all day he would go out at night. You can catch mullet like that. In between times he would catch fish. Each fish has its season: pompano has a season, mullet has a season, and mackerel has a season. Bud's first love was fishing although he did many other things. He kept coming back to fishing. If something else came up that he could make more money at, he would go do that, but would always come back to fishing."

We talked about her husband Bud whom I never met because he died the year before I moved to Marco. All the books she loaned me belonged to him.

"Bud had a great thirst for knowledge he read everything he could get his hands on," she explained. "He read books, but he spent all of his time researching out in the woods, looking for orchids, looking for other kinds of things. He was self-taught and self read."

Kappy and Bud lived in such an isolated place it made me wonder about what they did for doctors and hospitals, I suspected she went to Naples or Fort Myers, but didn't know.

"Was there a doctor on the island when you got pregnant?"

"No, we went to Miami."

"Miami? You went across the Tamiami Trail to Miami?"

"You see, I had a place to stay there. During the Depression Aunt Nona and Uncle Floy ran the Lodge for awhile. When things got better they moved to Miami and he got a job with the Marl Industries which was a cement place. He was just like a low person in the office who did book work. The first week he was there he found an error that saved them thousands of dollars a year. Because one truck was being loaded with a little bit more than it should have been, anyway it costs thousands of dollars in a year. He got a raise then and before he retired he was President of the Board of Marl Industries."

"They had a house and they bought a little restaurant with rooms upstairs. When I went to Miami to the doctor I would stay with my aunt. There were doctors in Fort Myers I suppose, but I probably didn't have a place to stay. I could stay with Aunt Nona."

"What happened when your time came?" I asked thinking of the many miles between the island and Miami on the other coast.

"I went to Miami however many times the doctor told me *to* come over and when the time came he would induce labor. I got too much fluid in my body with all three of my children."

"Edema?"

"Yes. So when I went over with each one of them, the doctor would say, 'Now it is time for you to go into the hospital.' With Damos I went over and was due to go back in six weeks. He said, 'Mrs. Kirk, I think you should go into the hospital now and not wait until next time.'"

"No, I can't. My daughter Kare is having a birthday party.'

"Well, I think you should go now."

"I repeated,' I can't my daughter is having a birthday party.'"

"Well, come just as soon as the birthday is over."

"Damos was the ugliest thing you ever saw in your life. He was just as red and wrinkled as he could be. His eyes were infected. I called him the 'Little Monster' when I talked to him. The nurses were furious with me for saying that to him. But, he was born with pneumonia.

"When we went back for the six weeks check up the doctor said, 'Well, his shoulder is healing nicely."

"What is wrong with his shoulder?"

"We had to break it to force delivery."

"It was just that close, but they didn't tell me that they broke his shoulder! It was actually his collarbone. He wasn't a big baby. Kare was 8 lbs. 4 oz., T.D. was a little lighter, and Damos was a little lighter.

"He had pneumonia. I guess he was probably drowning in fluids. He was a sickly little thing when we got him. He is fine now, he lost all that red and yellow look that he had in a few days. He was born with pneumonia and yellow jaundice."

"How did you go back and forth to Miami?"

"Let's see. The first car we had was just before we got married. Bud bought a little Ford, it was like a little convertible but it had the sides up, you could take the top down. Then, the next car we bought from Miami was a used car. The next one after that was a new Chevrolet. The next one after that was we had two Nashes, one small station wagon Nash, a yellow car with red seats, quite a combination, another station wagon a Chevrolet wore out in a year. The body was full of holes. I don't think we ever had a car more than a year. None of them had more than 45,000 miles on them before we traded them in. It was hard driving around here on the shell roads and the salt air made everything rusty. Then we had another little Nash that was a hideous color. Then we had a big Ford Station wagon. This is the last one I had."

"It took several weeks for the store to get all straightened out. I had the store temporarily in my house until it was finished."

"Harry Pettit told me the rattlesnakes used this pathway between my house and the store to go from low land to high land. I don't know if it was rainy season that they traveled or why they did it. But, they went from low land up into the 'Glades.

Rattlesnake   **Tommie D. about 2 & 1/2 yrs old**

"One time I was at the store with Carl Salo who was working on the shelves, when I looked out at my house which was just across the road. I saw Tommie Dee sitting on the front porch swinging her legs. The porch was still open then. Coming across right toward her feet was a four-foot rattlesnake. I almost had a heart attack. I yelled at Carl Salo who picked up some kind of tool and ran over to her. The snake went under the car and we never could find it to kill it. My heart pounded for hours after that. She was just sitting there with her feet moving, I know that snake would have attacked. It was a very hot time. She was two and a half. She and Kare were both at the house. I could see them, what was going on. The store was where Little Bar is now, but closer. You could walk right out of the front door of my house and to the store it was very close. There was no real road for the house.

"We had no electricity, no water, no telephone, nothing but a dear old piece of land. We had a bathroom that we couldn't use, there was no plumbing. We built an outside privy and had an outhouse for a short time.

"We had a little old building from somewhere, made of plastic. We took an oil drum and put diesel fuel in for the electricity. It was enough power to run the lights and one unit at a time. So, when you went in the early morning, you'd put the drink box on, when that got cold you'd run out take that off and put another thing on. We were running back and forth to keep the electrical appliances running. The generator house was behind the store. We have a picture of it. Anyway, I had to run back and forth all day to switch it. It had a little motor and could only cool one coke-a-cola box at a time.

Shed and Fishnets

"Tell me about the fish nets I see in the picture."

"When we first came to Goodland we also brought our fishermen. Most of the people who lived at Caxambas were fishermen. A couple of them guided in season, but most earned their living from fishing, primarily mullet fishing. Because that is what you use these kinds of nets for. Sometimes it might have been a pompano net, Bud was a pompano fisherman. When we came over here we called this a *commercial fishing village,* because most of the people made their living by the sea. Not any more because restrictions have been put on fishing and bans on net fishing. The fish are not as plentiful as they were. That makes it very difficult to make a living from fishing.

"I think Bud might have gotten the shed out in the middle of the island where Colliers were going to put a building that they were going to furnish electricity for. Those things are in Caxambas and Marco, it was completely built, but it was never used for electricity. It was abandoned and the Colliers were planning to give it to Bud... but it burned down. When we first moved here there were no houses in Goodland, no people lived here. There was just the white house on the right that belonged to Charley Shaffer beside Harry Pettit. On the shore, we called the shore the bank, the fishermen would dry their nets on racks. The nets were made of cotton threads. When you pulled up fish, the slime from the nets would rot the nets. The fishermen used lime to clean them. They put lime and poured water on them in the well of the boat, wash the slime from the nets, then rinse them and put them out to dry on the racks. After we came the little village of Goodland had twenty houses and all would all have net racks and nets drying, that was their livelihood. All those were handmade nets. They bought what they called trammel, made the nets, and sewed the cork lines and the lead lines on the nets."

"This net looks whiter than the others."

"That might be a newer net. Now, pompano nets would be off shore and they might be whiter, but the fishermen didn't dye their nets. Discolored nets would indicate the age of the net, slightly discolored."

"Your property extended behind the shed?"

"Yes, the bay back there was eventually filled in some. That is where the fish house is now. The home next to the white house was moved from Caxambas. The fish house was already there. That is what Bud and I rented."

CHAPTER 4

Caxambas

Caxambas Village

"When we were in Caxambas we had a power plant. When I say Caxambas I don't mean that part of the island we now called the *Estates*, I mean the little village of Caxambas that was just about as big as you see in the picture, it went from the water line all the way back to where the Charlie Griner property, where Otter Mound Park; remember that was Aunt Tommie's and Uncle Jim's property, they helped him buy the property.

"Pat Leo had the power plant fixed up. You will notice the power poles in the picture. We had electric lines coming in to the houses. Some houses in the other section weren't electrified and they used kerosene lamps. Our section and the store had electricity so it was very different when coming over here to Goodland without any electricity at all. It was a challenge! You had to be made out of real strong stuff in order to survive.

"Pat also had a water system hooked up. The water was fresh, especially in the rainy season, but sometimes in the dry season it would get brackish so that you couldn't drink it. You could take baths in it and wash in it. You could cook with it if you added other water to it. It would get quite salty.

"Harry Pettit owned all the property in Goodland before he sold it, and one of his brothers lived in Caxambas also. When we came over to Goodland there was just Harry and two other people that lived here. There were some cottages. A man named Ed Scott who worked for the post office and now lives in another part of the state had a fishing cottage he used. But that was all the people living here. There weren't that many boats in the harbor. So when the move came the fishermen brought their boats and spread their nets out."

Scripts School and Playground

"There was no school in Goodland. The children still went to Scripts School in Caxambas. It was located on a hill on the Ludlow property. It is about where the Tateo property above where Olds Court is now. Up until they built the Scripps school each village, Caxambas and Marco, had its own school. When they built Scripps School they consolidated the two schools. It was a two-story cement building and had four classrooms in it. It had high ceilings and large windows. The lower grades were in the ground floor classrooms. The upper grades were upstairs. There was a school bus that picked up the children from Marco and from Caxambas.

Faye Weeks Brown wrote about a school bus accident when Uncle Johnny, Tommie's brother, was the driver for Scripp School, "One day as we were on our way home from school, we had a wreck. I was in the first grade at the time. Uncle Johnny Stephen's was the bus driver. He wasn't my uncle that is just what everyone called him. I think he may have driven the bus when our mama was in school there. Anyway, we were bounding up and down on our seats as the bus was traveling the rough limestone and oyster shell road across the san hills of Caxambas when all of a sudden, as we turned a sharp hill, going down through the narrow road that was a short distance through mangrove swamps;' we struck a car that was parked on the narrow road and veered off a five foot high embankment into the swamp.

"All of the kids had to be pulled out the back emergency door because the front door of the bus was partially buried in the salt muck and mangrove trees. I was thrown about ten feet under the seats and struck my side on the metal legs. The kids were a little dazed but started to walk toward the cross roads. I cannot remember how we got home but word must have reached the village and cars came to pick up the children. Yvonne Cook was cut n her arm pretty badly. Some tourist stopped and gave her a lift over the sand bank on Smoke House bay. A retired doctor by the name of Campbell lived on a lighter there. He had to pick sticks out of her wound before stitching it up. The superintendent came to everyone's home to see if they were o.k. Some tourist parked a car on the narrow road to watch the raccoons on the oyster shell banks in the swamp there. We watched them every day as the bus went by, they turned the oyster shell over and picked the small crabs off to eat. Maybe that is why they call the small oysters coon oysters."

The children attended Scripps founded in 1928 until the Tommie Barfield Elementary School was built in 1956, twenty-eight years later.

"It is hard to imagine in some ways there was very little change. The children, Bud and I were still living in the same house, we had the same friends, and even the customers in the store were all the same, because we all moved over. Nothing was left in Caxambas but a few families who owned their properties and did not sell to the Colliers. Most everything and everybody came over here. We just moved to another location."

"Our refrigerator was run by kerosene oil. It would keep things cold in the house but not the store. The range was propane.

"It was the worst trial we ever went through, it was dreadful. It was almost like being on an island out in the middle of the Pacific. Everything was hard. The shell that was pushed four feet over to level it off was plain white shell, no trees or shrubs. It was hot. Hot as the dickens. No electricity, no water, and it was hot. It lasted two years or more."

"What did you do for water?"

"Eventually, Mr. Dickerson, a man who owned that blue building had a truck with a tank on it, brought it in. We'd get water from him a tank full at a time. Then we built a cistern under the garage about eight feet deep, it holds about 3,000 gallons. Not everyone dug cisterns, some caught it in rain barrels from the eaves of the house and some bought it from Mr. Dickerson. We did what we had to do, we made do.

"When Damos was born, eleven years after Kare, every afternoon we'd put on our bathing suits, get our soap, our wash cloths and towels and go over to Marco to the Marco Lake to swim and take our baths. They dug a hole on Marco Lake Drive creating a fresh water lake. Damos learned to swim underwater over there. I can remember that we'd be on one shore and there was a four-foot alligator on the opposite shore. He swam over there and we swam over on our side, neither one of us bothering the other. We both wanted water. Then after we had our bath and got nice and cool; we'd get in the car and drive slowly out to Royal Palm Hammock or out to the beach. We'd sing and that was our visiting time. When we came home the house was cooled off and we could sleep. It was a very pleasant part of our lives at that time."

"What did you use for the bathroom?"

"We used an outside privy, we had a bathroom in the house but you couldn't use it. The Colliers' tried desperately to get fresh water for us. They drilled wells that went 2,500 feet deep eventually looking for water. They had what they called Tampa strata where the natural rock formation flows and the fresh water flows from the north of us. They have good water in Everglades. They'd go down to 250 feet and the salt water would seep in from the top. They'd go deeper and the salt water would come in from the bottom. They would get salt in it and you couldn't drink it. We used it to cook with because it was salty, not salty, but brackish. Cooking and cleaning.

"We had dinner early because the smell of food cooking would bring mosquitoes. We didn't need extra ones!

"We'd get the kitchen cleaned up, get our bath and get on our pajamas on, as I told you, take a long ride to the beach or Royal Palm Hammock; they would be tired and sleepy and ready for bed when we got home. Everything was cooled down, they went to bed without a murmur, we were ready to go to sleep too. You do what you have to do."

"The Colliers did everything that you could ask to be done and they did it because they felt the responsibility of their father's promise."

I felt at this point that I had to ask her about some of the rumors against the Collier Corporation that had come to me. "I've heard Goodland residents, especially the new ones, talk about the Colliers' taking advantage of people, of moving people out of Caxambas, how they just took everything and moved everyone over here."

I've heard that for years and years," Kappy responded, "but it is not true. It definitely isn't true. People didn't own their houses in Caxambas, they didn't own their property, when they came over here they became property holders with a lot and a house. The Colliers made it easy for them to buy. I think the lowest piece of property for them to buy was $300. A place to put your house with the house put on there at no expense. No down payment, and three years to pay the house off. They have done everything they said they would do. I was close enough to know what was going on to KNOW that was true."

"What were the Colliers going to do with that property after everyone was moved out?"

"I've heard several different stories, but this is the one that I think is true. Some of those men lived over there almost free one man paid 50 cents for his rent. We paid fifteen dollars a month for this house. It was about as expensive as anyone paid over there. Rex Johnson lived in back of my house in a little trailer park over there. Rex would run down and say Kirk Bowers was doing something he didn't like, and others would complain about other things. I think they just got tired of it.

"Then there was talk about offshore drilling, a place they could bring in oil. They didn't want those cottages there they needed them off of there. That was one thing. Then there was another story that said they were getting everybody off of there so that if they started to develop they wouldn't have a problem, they could just go ahead and develop. It might have been one or all of the reasons, why they moved at that particular time. They'd run over to Everglades and complain. "

"Did the Colliers' do anything else for the residents besides dig the wells?"

"Well, that was an expensive operation. Besides that, they did level the top four feet of ground. They didn't have to do that, they didn't have to do any of it. They could have said get out. They could have given the houses to people and said you have thirty days to get the house off the property. They were not bound legally in anyway. It was their property.

"These few houses were made of heart of village pine from the 1910 hurricane. Come on and I will show you what the lumber looks like. Mr. Pettit was just living here with a few men around, it was probably lonely here. I think he probably enjoyed the people coming from Caxambas, he had sold the property years ago."

Becoming Postmaster

"No one ever wanted to be postmaster, there was practically no money in it at all. It was a job passed around in the Barfield family for a long time. In 1937 Elva Barfield was postmaster we still have her cashbook in one quarter, in three months she made $92.00. The way you made the money, you took a certain percentage of the stamp sales that you made, that one quarter. You had to be here every day, everything that one does now and one did back then. You sold stamps, you had a big mail order business, and practically everything that came onto the island was bought from Sears or Montgomery Ward Catalogue stores. You'd have packages come in COD from Atlanta. You'd put the notices in the mailbox, then when people came in they brought you the money, then you made the money order and would send it back to the company. We'd keep the merchandise there in the store. It had a tag, you took the tag off and they signed it, then they'd give you the money. The Post office would make out the money order and mail it back to them. We'd buy everything: clothing, shoes, sheets, pillowcases, dishtowels, and everything you'd buy now.

Turning a Turtle at the Old Marco Village

"There was a beautiful swimming beach where the ferry approach was, where the historical marker is now in Marco. If you are standing there look straight across to your left to the shoreline on the extreme West. The Isles of Capri community across the river was not there at this time. There was a nice big beach with shallow water it was a lovely place to swim. We used to go over there and have picnics. We had gone over there to see if we could turn a turtle. When your turn a turtle over he is yours. The turtles would come up there to lay their eggs. People would go out. At that time, anything you found was actually like food. You were breaking the law nobody cared because you weren't doing any real damage to the economy or the ecosystem. I think that was the reason we went over that day, there were about fifteen people on boats who all went over to go swimming, picnicking, and try to turn a turtle.

"They actually turned it over on its back and it was helpless. They would kill it and take the good parts from it. All the people would take a share of it and take it home and cook it for themselves.

"I tried to eat turtle eggs but I didn't like them. They were coarse, they didn't taste like eggs. People would take a few, a long time ago, but they didn't destroy things. They took what they needed. They killed curlew that is the white Ibis. If you had three in the family, he brought one curlew home, we ate the breast and the legs, the rest of it, was put into a pot and you made a stew out of it. People were not destructive.

"People who came down here for visits would bring lots and lots of jars of food, meat, or greens or what have you. They would eat the food and then they had an empty jar so they went out and got oysters and clams, birds, fish and whatever they could get. They would fill that jar up, can it and take it home. You can't say that they were stingy they were just poor people who came down here and camped during the wintertime. At home they worked like dogs in the summer time. I'm not saying anything bad about them they just lived off of the land. Much as the natives did. But more so, because the natives took only what they could use at the present time, these people took a lot of things for the future. The local people didn't like the first people that came down here as campers because as I say they practically lived off of the land. They had a saying that 'people come down here and they have a blue shirt and a five dollar bill and they don't change either one of them until they get back home.'"

"When I say I am going to town, I mean I'm going to Fort Myers or Miami, because that is where we went shopping. In 1949 we could drive the Trail, the Tamiami Trail of course. We bought staples that would last us a month, canned things and bags of things that you could keep for a long time.

"We kept the grocery store going until we sold it around 1951 to Elva. We sold it for $6,000. She didn't want it for anything special it was just a good buy. She kept it for awhile.

"That was when Bud and I had marital problems. I divorced him for awhile, at that time I hated him, I really did. I said you get your clothes together and I am taking you to Miami and you can go anywhere you damn well please. I couldn't stand to look at him. I think it was a combination of moving over here, and all the problems we had to face. Bud would go off fishing when I really truly needed him at home. He would get drunk and when he did that, I hated him. It was a combination of that and all the other. I don't like excessive drinking. Bud was not a drunkard, but when he started drinking it would go on until he got drunk. The next day he'd get sober, it was more than I could put up with. I think if it were a normal situation, I could have handled it, but the stress of living here, there were too many things. That was the straw that broke the camel's back.

"We were separated for about six months. I took the children and we went to Pennsylvania where I had some friends. Bud was staying with his aunt in Massachusetts. I said that I would put the children on a train and send them for a visit. He said no, that I would have to bring them over there. So I did. I left my car at my friend's house and we all went by train. Bud met me at the train.

"Kappy, let's go talk," he said

"Bud, I don't think we have anything to talk about."

He said, "Let's go back together."

"No Bud, I've had enough of you."

He said, "Kappy, I promise that I will not drink anymore."

"Do you *swear* you won't drink anymore?"

"We went back together and it worked out. He didn't drink for seven years. Then when he drank, he still drank to get drunk, but he was careful about it.

"Life wasn't easy for anyone. He fished and guided and took people out in the boat. Our house became a place to ask for information. If anyone came on the island and asked anything about the birds around here, people would recommend asking Bud Kirk about it, he could tell them. Someone came and asked about orchids, flowers, fish whatever it was people were always dropping by. Of course the fishermen always had their buddies over for coffee when they came off the boats. So the house was just a meeting place for everybody, which I liked.

"I never knew whom I would find. This one particular time I had a black man who worked at the water plant in Marco, two or three fishermen with their rubber boots on and this one particular day was unusual because Dr Henry Field author of *The Track of Man* of Chicago was there. Dr. Field did the anthropology part of the Fields Museum of Chicago, had brought a Russian prince! That stayed in my mind longer than anything else did, because I hadn't ever entertained a Russian prince before. They were all sitting around the table and went into the dining room because they couldn't all get around the kitchen table."

"When Bud was forty years old, ten years after were married, he said, 'You know Kappy, I think I would have been a lot happier if I had gone to school.' He left school in the ninth grade when he left home.

"I said to him, 'Bud - there is no reason why you can't go to school if you want to. I think Dr. Henry Field was here when we were talking about it. Dr. Field said, 'Bud, I have a nice little cottage on my property, made out of native stone. There is not a soul in it. You can stay in it as long as you like and go to school.'

"So Bud went to school for a year. He came back with 4.0 grades, a straight A student. As a matter of fact when we go through my boxes, I have an article that Betty Bruno wrote about a boy, fresh out of high school, going to college, who was in a couple of classes with Bud. He said that when he went on a Botany class field trip, he was sure to get in the car with Bud and Dr. Irie. He said, 'I learned more listening to Bud and Dr. Irie talk in that car than I learned in school.' Bud was a smart boy, if he had worked on it he could have been anything he wanted to be. He knew a lot about Anthropology, Archaeology, all that. Bud found some Spanish things over here on Marco Island. He found a clay pipe in the area of Cape Romano, actually Tommie Dee found it. Bud found a very nice little clay pot about so big, all the pieces are there, some day someone needs to put them all together. John Beriault, a vocational archaeologist who worked with Bob Carr on digs around here, used to sit out in the yard and talk for hours about things."

Chapter 5
The Movie

"Bud actually started drinking again when the movie people came, but it was different, he didn't' make a complete ass of himself."

"Tell me how Bud met Budd Shulberg the author of the book *Wind Across the Everglades*."

"Let me start by telling you what Bud was doing at the time. Bud was fishing then. The fishermen were almost like nomads depending on what kind of fish they were trying to catch. The mullet season was in October or November. The old time fishermen used to say that they were going out to catch their *Christmas Money*. The fishermen gathered in the lower Matacombe Keys, they had moored their boat there and took the fish in to sell. Bud and his crewmen had gone into a grocery store, one end of which had a little bar that sold beer. Bud was in there having his lunch"

"Over in the corner was a man kind of grumbling to himself about the couple sitting at the bar. This man said to himself, 'Don't allow no g__ d__ Arabs in this place.'

"When he got a little bit louder, Bud finally said quietly to him, 'Alright, that is enough of that. You just calm down or I am going to throw you out of here."

"Then Bud went back and sat down and said to people at the bar, 'My name is Bud Kirk.'

"Budd Shulberg introduced himself and his wife and they got to talking.

"Bud said, 'Shulberg? Oh yes, I've just read a book by a man named Shulberg, *What Makes Sammy Run*.'

"Budd Shulberg turned to his wife and stuttered, 'M-M-mama, this raggedy old F-F-fisherman has r-read my b-book'

"They started talking, Shulberg who was from New York state, wanted to know about everything, he found it very exciting. They talked about Bud Kirk having worked on the Audubon Society boat as a game warden. The more they talked Bud Shulberg began to sense that the things Bud Kirk said were something any man would have like to have done. He pulled a match book out of his pocket and wrote Bud Kirk, Goodland on it. He carried it around for so many years that he began to wear off the last name, but he knew the first name was Bud. He wrote a post card to 'Bud Kirk at Goodland' and to 'Bud Collier' at Naples. At that time there was a man on television whose name was Collier. Bud Kirk received both cards here in Goodland. There were so few people in Naples, Marco, Chokoluskee, and Everglades, that he knew almost everybody. He got the cards. I don't remember what it said; Bud got in touch with him.

"They came down and they started thinking about this play that he had written. He wrote a play and sent it down to Bud to go over to find any mistakes and errors in the script. Bud went over it and made some 125 corrections in it.

"Shulberg said, 'Are you sure Bud?' Bud began telling him about what the errors were and he used every one of them except one."

I could hardly believe what Kappy was telling me that her husband Bud inspired the famous movie *Wind Across the Everglades* about plume hunters and an Autobahn warden. I remember seeing the movie in my hometown in Duncan, Oklahoma.

"What happened after that? How did they take it from a screen play to production?" I asked rather skeptically.

"Shulberg wanted Bud to play the good guy, the Audubon warden. Bud said, 'No, I don't want to do that!' Shulberg asked, 'Will you be the technical director?' Bud agreed, he'd be happy to. The movie was mostly made in Everglades and they rented apartments for people to stay, all the crew to stay. The movie was named *Wind Across the Everglades,* with Christopher Plummer, as the Audubon Warden (Bud's part), Beryl Ives as Cotton Mouth, the villain of the piece, Emmett Kelly, the famous circus clown, played a member of Cotton Mouth's gang, Totch Brown, a well known Everglade local, was also a gang member. Corey Ocseola the Indian Chief was the one Bud had to teach acting lessons to. Gypsy Rose Lee, famous night club stripper, played the part of a Madame. The movie as written by Bud Shulberg and directed by his brother Stuart Shulberg"

Christopher Plummer

Burl Ives

Emmett Kelly

Corey Osceola

Gypsy Rose Lee

Kappy pulled out an autographed picture of Stuart and said, "Let me read what Stuart Shulberg and his brother wrote on the picture:

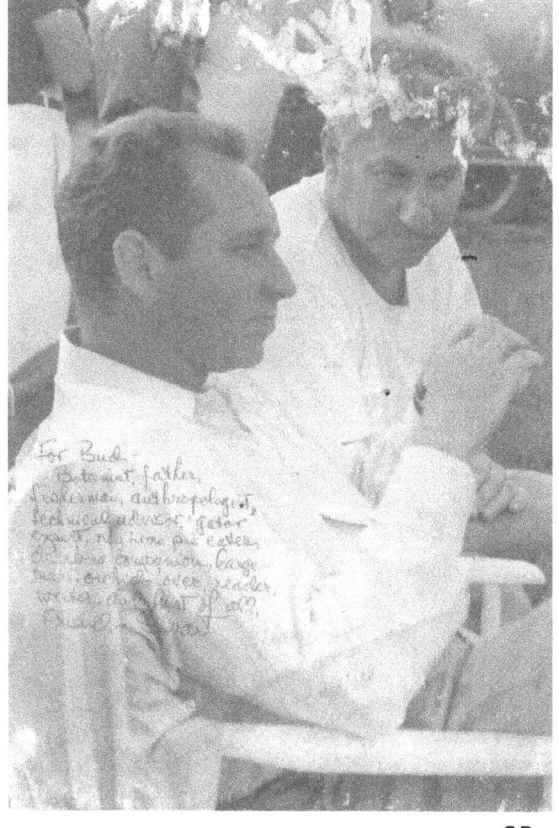

**The Shulbergs
Stuart
(Left)
Budd
(Right)**

To Bud, fisherman, anthropologist, technical advisor, gator expert, key lime pie-eater, drinking companion, large man, orchid lover, reader, writer, and best of all, Friend.' Stuart Shulberg.

Dear Bud, I knew you'd finally patronize me by asking for my autograph. You've taught me a lot, I hope this picture does you justice. Always, Budd.'

"These pictures went through hurricane Donna and show a little wear on the top," Kappy said.

"My husband Bill will have to work a little of his computer magic to touch them up and repair them," I replied, a firm believer at this point.

"Here is a newspaper article from the regional scene Naples Daily News from July 8, 1979, a picture of Corey Osceola, as Seminole Chief, Peter Falk as the bad guy, Budd Shulberg the author, Gypsy Rose Lee, stripper."

Naples Daily News, July 8, 1979

Gypsy Rose Lee

"Tell me about Gypsy," I said looking at the old clipping.

"She arrived in Everglades City in a pink Rolls Royce. She had her pets with her, twenty-eight cats."

"Twenty-eight cats?"

"Yes. She had to take two rooms at the Rod and Gun Club, one for herself and one room for her cats. They weren't too happy about it, but that's what she did.

"She was quite a gal, she fit right in with that group. Once they were getting out of a boat, they had to climb up a ladder to reach the dock because it was low tide it was quite a distance to climb up this ladder to get off-board. Gypsy had on a wrap around skirt and Bud was holding the ladder, helping her get on the dock. Her skirt flew open and exposed her rear-all of it. Bud caught his breath, 'Eh!'

"Gypsy said to him, 'What's the matter Bud, haven't you ever seen a lady's ass before?'"

"She must of been quite a character."

"She was!"

Movie Truck

"There were quite a few of the locals in the movie. Everglades City was their headquarters, but it was actually shot down toward the Keys, Shark River, and Flamingo. They brought all that equipment on trucks, heavy cameras and such here to Marco Island to do their beach scene. Then they went off to check something else. I guess it was a Saturday because I wasn't working that day. I was there on the beach with them. This big piece of equipment on a truck was parked close to the water's edge. As the tide started coming in the sand would get soft and they'd have a hard time moving that truck out of there.

"All the people around there were just the technicians and the movie people at the moment. I was watching the tide, finally I said, 'That truck's got to be moved, pretty soon, the tide will come in and you won't be able to get it out.' No one did anything; they just stood there. I repeated, 'You'd better get that truck, that piece of equipment out because you'll lose it'"

"They kind of looked off and acted as if they didn't hear me or want to hear me. Finally I said, 'Look, it has to be moved!' Then one man mumbled, 'Well, we're only technicians here we're not truck drivers, we're not allowed to touch those trucks, we can't move that truck.'

"Exasperated with that kind of logic, I said, 'Well, I can touch the truck. I'll get the damn thing out! I started over to sit in the truck and the men started coming over. I showed him how to back it up and get it on higher ground. That is a true story."

"Here is a picture of Peter Falk, with a beard 1957-58, was he one of the bad guys."

"Kappy, I don't remember him in the movie, I may not have recognized him. You have a poster here that you made with four large pictures missing of Corey Osceola, Emmett Kelly, Gypsy Rose Lee, and Christopher Plummer as well as some smaller snapshots of Burl Ives, and Peter Falk. On the other side are Corey Osceola and Kare Kirk! Your daughter was in the movie? You're kidding!"

"She was in the crowd scenes. This is Charles McGuire assistant director who took over on the second half of the movie after Stuart died.

"This is Chana Eden, co-star, the lovely new European actress, all dressed up with a feather boa and hat. She played the part of the warden's female interest."

"This newspaper-clipping reads 'starts today, Bud Shulberg's *Wind Across the Everglade*s, a Florida you never knew about, mysterious, dark and deadly.'"

"Someone sent us that."

Technicolor. Here's Tony Galento, heavy weight fighter, as "Beef" the escaped convict; McKinley Cantor, the celebrated author, as the gin-soaked swamp judge; Christopher Plummer, the one man who dared go into the swamp after Cottonmouth; Emmett Kelly, the famous circus clown, as "Bigamy Bob," the many times married outlaw; and Sammy Remick, the famous jockey, named "Loser", a renegade from the track.

"Here is a picture of Stuart Shulberg's son shaking hands with Christopher Plummer," He was one of my favorite actors after seeing *The Sound of Music*. "What was Christopher Plummer like?" I asked.

"He was charming. He fit right into this house when he had dinner with us. He got up to help Kare take the dishes off the table. He was a perfect person.

"On set Tommie Dee, Damos and Bud were all in the train on a set. A film personnel noted, 'one without shoes' that was Bud, he was infamous for going without shoes.

"Sheriff Doug Hendry, Joe Hunter and Aubrey Rogers were in the movie too."

Newspaper article

Gypsy Rose Lee rolled into town into EC in a pink Rolls with 28 cats. She did an impromptu strip tease on the Kirk's boat just off of Clam Slough now know as Tigertail Beach. Her wrap around skirt fell off. Journalistic license made it more dramatic. The helmsman eyes popped out like door knobs. *Whatsa matta kid, ain't you seen a lady strip before?* Bud Kirk put up with a lot of that and other things as he served as technical director for the first movie and perhaps the last ever shot in Collier County.

"This is a cassette recording of the movie, a rather poor recording," she added holding up the small black cassette, "I thought the movie was pretty good when it first came out," said Kappy.

"Oh," I said holding it in my hands like a fragile artifact, "I thought it was a wonderful movie. I was so impressed with the movie; when you said it was made about your husband…I looked at you and thought…"

"You thought she's just full of it," Kappy quipped and we both laughed out loud.

"You surely proved me wrong backing it up with all this proof about meeting Budd Shulberg and then everyone else who came down and made the movie. Do you have anything else to tell me about that time?"

"Well, it was exciting. Perhaps I shouldn't say this, but there was only one person who was full of herself. She thought she was above all the ratty fishermen around here and that was Peter Falk's wife. If she wanted anything she drove up in her little convertible and beeped the horn for someone to come out. You can see me out there running out there?

"She was on location with him?" I said trying to imagine it.

"Yes."

"Was Christopher Plummer married?"

"Yes, but his wife wasn't with him. He thought my daughter Kare was such a great girl. He said anytime she needs to go to higher education, he'd love to have her come up and stay with them. I think he was living in Canada at that time. And he was a charming down to earth kind of person; I enjoyed having him here."

"Burl Ives, did you ever…?"

"Oh yeah," she said shrugging her shoulders.

"You don't think much of Burl Ives?"

"Burl <u>could sing</u>. He was a kind of all bluster… scared to death of everything out in the glades. He was scared of snakes."

"In the movie he had a snake he was supposed to carry around with him."

"I remember, he carried it in his pocket, which is why he was called Cottonmouth: it was a poisonous snake."

"No, it was not poisonous, it was just a little harmless black snake.

"Anyway, they had to take out a two million-dollar life insurance on him before he would come down in the first place. Bud had the job of trying to get him to handle that snake; he couldn't get him to touch it. One time, Bud was invited to have dinner with him at his cottage. And when he got there, Burl poured out a drink of whiskey and he poured an 8-ounce glass of vodka or something strong like an Irish whiskey for Bud to drink. And Bud looked at him and said, 'I'm not that kind of man, I don't drink like that.' He took a sip. Burl was trying to show off. He drank a water glass not a shot glass of whiskey.

"So…Bud tried to teach him to touch that snake. It was just a little harmless black snake, but he wouldn't touch it. Finally, Bud said to himself, 'I'm going to get him to handle that snake.' So he came to wherever his house was to Burl and Burl said, 'Ok, I'm ready to handle that snake.'

"Bud said, 'No, you are not ready yet.'

"'What do you mean I'm not ready?'

"'I'll tell you when you are ready.' He would not let him handle it for a good long while, but just teased him around it. Finally, Burl grabbed hold of it, but it took a long time."

"So Bud used reverse psychology on Burl?"

"Yes, to make him *want* to take the snake. So he finally got him to take the snake. The cast and crew didn't all stay at the Rod and Gun Club, there was a little motel over there where people stayed and there was a boarding house where some of the people stayed."

The Manchineel Tree!

"It was a tree that put out a poisonous sap on the tree. I guess if a person had enough of that sap on them it would finally kill them. It starts out like blistering your skin. Anyway, in one of the scenes the Indian was being punished for a crime and they were going to tie him to one of the Manchineel trees. He was supposed to scream out, 'no NO… NOT the Manchineel tree!'

"Bud had a terrible time getting him to scream, because Indians talk very softly, very gently. Finally, he got him to cry, 'not the manchineel tree' but it wasn't a very big scream."

"That was Corey Osceola and his part? "I asked.

"Yes. I think that Corey Osceola was the one that Aunt Tommie took to New York to the World's Fair. She took him to see a movie. He had never been to a movie before. It was a cowboy picture, when the cowboy shot the Indian Corey stood up and cried, 'No, white man kill Indian, Me kill white man!'"

"'Sh, sh, sit down, sit down, sit down, sit down. It's alright. Sit down,' Aunt Tommie said." She took him to the World's Fair to see and be seen.

"This was an article in the newspaper about the movie."

The movie was written for Warner Brothers by Budd Shulberg, author of "What makes Sammy Run" and "On the Waterfront." It was about egret hunters in Florida. Stuart was director; he had esteemed Bud Kirk ever since a half-baked fisherman was poking a knife into Shulberg's belly. Also he admired the self learned Kirk for educated that he had picked up in Botany, Archaeology and History while fishing for mackerel and running a clam factory. Thanks to Bud Kirk the movie went on schedule. Burl Ives played the two-ton bad guy. Tony G. a henchman, Peter Falk who wore a beard then and went on to 'Columbo' was a bad guy too. Kelly the clown was a plume hunter. Gypsy Rose Lee was the Madame of a Miami sporting house where the plume hunters spent their ill-gotten gains. Seminole Chief also had a part. Christopher Plummer was the heroic Audubon warden sent to stop the slaughter of the birds.

The cast stayed at the Rod and Gun Club during the shooting and Gypsy needed an extra room for her cats. It all came back to Bud Kirk and his wife Kappy when Stuart S. died in New York this week. "The family asked Bud Kirk to deliver the eulogy at the last rites. Budd Shulberg said, "Kirk had the eloquence of Thoreau."

Kappy added, "A famous man on radio or TV spoke before Bud went on, afterwards came over and shook Bud's hand and said, 'I wish I'd have said that.'"

"Bud stayed over quite a bit. At night they would go down to Copeland. There was a big store that was one of the fun places to go. After dinner all the group met in Copeland, what did they call it... I guess it was just a bar. They went on until about 2:00 in the morning. Then at 6:00 a.m. they were yelling, 'time to get up.' They lived hard. It was mostly the movie people, set people, actors, locals like us, the whole bunch. Party all night and get up."

"Well some of the drunken scenes looked like they were really drunk."

"I wouldn't be surprised."

Bud Kirk

"Chana Eden, that pretty girl from France would attack almost anything in pants. I was a little annoyed with her. I wouldn't call it jealous, just annoyed. All Bud would have to do was curl his finger for her to come."

"Bud was a good looking man. There were other actors there?"

"I don't think it would have made a difference to her, what they looked like."

"The movie was finished in 1959. Bud Shulberg gave him the marine plywood left over from the movie. He took that and built the Goodland Post Office. We had a dedication of the post office and took pictures."

Hurricane Donna, 1960

"But the post office didn't last long. In 1960 Hurricane Donna came along and blew a trailer from across the street, which took the roof off and knocked it 16 feet off the foundation."

Hurricane Donna a Category 4 storm

"It wasn't good anymore, so Bud cleaned that debris off and built another post office. That is the one we have now."

"I was head of the Red Cross at the time. Sixty people were ordered to evacuate to Naples High School in Naples. I didn't want to go but they said, 'Kappy, if you don't go, no one will.' We sat up tables there and I made coffee all night. During the worst of the storm the roof rose and fell. Once there was a loud crash behind where I was sitting. The people were scared too and panicky saying, 'Kappy, we have to leave, get out of here.' I knew I had to remain calm because I had been through hurricanes before and they all knew it. I tried to calm things down and just told them it would be all right even though the hair on the back of my neck rose.

"After the storm we went back to Goodland finding a huge tree as big as a man down, and all the telephone poles. Most of it was covered with water, Old Nanny Hudson, didn't leave and was sitting in her kitchen sink with the water just ready to come over the sink when the water went down. She wasn't actually in the sink, the dog was in the sink, the parakeet was on top of the refrigerator and Nanny was perched on the drain board. Her daughter Kathleen was on the table that nearly started floating. The house itself was floating held in place only by the front steps and back steps. Nanny said she could see a huge big grey wall of water coming."

"'I'll never stay again,' she said.

"Many roofs were taken off with homes and businesses destroyed during that horrible storm with 150 mph winds.

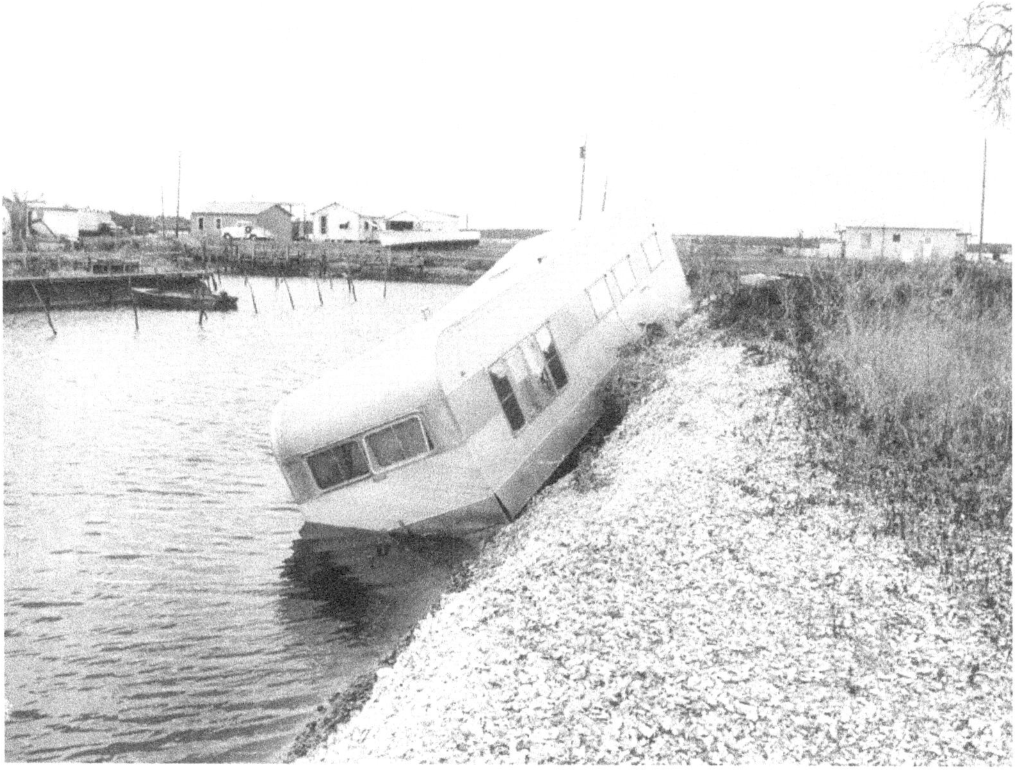

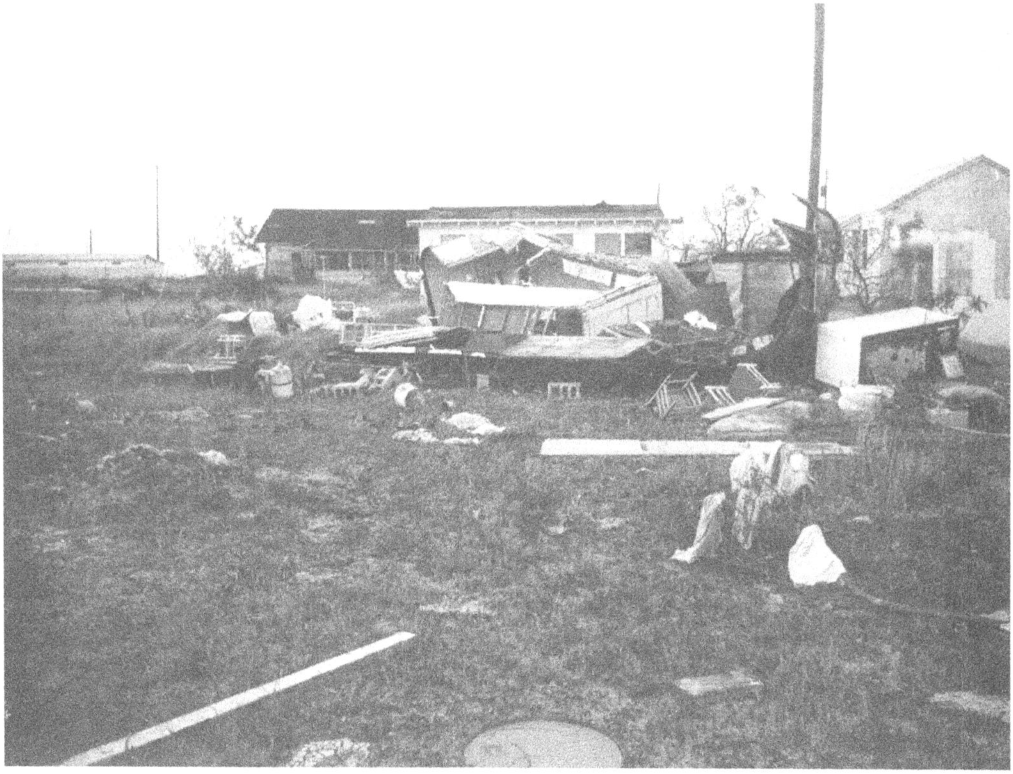

Wind gusts up to 175 mph blew trailer homes away or tossed them like tin cans.

It hurt Marco too, Camilla Rimes Kevetko, Jewel Weeks, and Pearl Vickers in the ruin of her home.

Doxsee Trailer Park

Damaged Boats

My house with the U S Post Office Goodland, P.O. Hours 9 – 5 pm, No mail service except posted hours above. Please Mail arrives at 9:50 pm, departs for all points at 5:00pm

"My home on top of the shell mound was the only dry place, so that became the community center. My daughter's bedroom was the Red Cross office, the fire place was the post office, and the front porch was where we distributed meals. I had never changed and still cooked with propane. My sister in Naples had a big freezer full of venison, turkey, fish and other things to eat. I must have cooked 350 meals, I was so tired at night and dropped in bed.

"Hurricane Donna hit Everglades City also and did a lot of damage, it wiped out Deaconess Bedell's mission."

CHAPTER 6
Deaconess Bedell (1875 -1969)
Missionary to the Indians, Everglades, Florida

Deaconess Bedell

Deaconess Harriet Bedell was a missionary to the Indians of the Everglades and began working with them in 1933. Deaconess had a cottage in Everglades City that she named Glades Cross Mission as her headquarters. She did not offer them charity; she encouraged them to help themselves, to develop their arts and crafts and sell their artifacts outside of Everglades. Her mission "became a wholesale and a retail center for

Seminole products such as: Bookends, dolls, pot-holders, baskets of all sizes, Seminole clothing, plaques, broom holders, aprons, miniature canoes, and palmetto placemats to mention a few. She established a branch of the mission in Immokalee to sell alligator, deer, and coon hides. One feature of this 30 foot by 20 foot mission was a 20 by 20 space marked off for a sick room. Eight of the 27 Indians in camp came down with the measles the following year, with medicine obtained from a white doctor, she helped them recover.

Glades Cross Mission 1947 – 48, Faye Seamon, Fred 7mos, George 4 yrs on right (photo courtesy of Faye Seaman)

The Mikasukis Indians lived in the huge Cypress Swamp in villages sometimes 10 to 15 miles apart, her medical aid as well as her economic aid won the confidence of the whole tribe.

They honored her by attending her Christmas parties with a decorated tree and feast followed by handing out gifts such as board games for the children or dominoes, rattles for the babies, blankets for the women, and shot gun shells for the men.

Seminole family next to the Mission sign (photo courtesy of Faye Seaman)

Deaconess also worked with the pioneer families of Everglades, Caxambas, & Goodland (photo courtesy of Faye Seamon)

The Deaconess came to Goodland to teach Sunday school and had sewing classes. Kappy helped her in all things and knew her very well.

"I've heard you tell a story the Deaconess and your honeymoon. What's that about?" I asked.

"Well, we got married at the Catholic Church in Fort Myers in 1941 and we had a big reception at Marco in the afternoon. It was a countywide reception, Aunt Tommie knew everyone. Mr. Freeman, Aunt Tommie's cook, baked the wedding cake. When he put the cake on the card table, the only thing you could see of the table was just about an inch or two around the edges. It was that big… it took him a week to make it. He fed two hundred guests at Marco Lodge. The Lodge was still in Marco at the time.

"After the reception we planned to go down to Shark River in Bud's boat. The boat was tied at the Goodland Bridge. So when we left the Lodge we got to the little cattle gap that kept Aunt Tommie's pigs and cows from getting into the village (Aunt Tommie's farm is now Mackle Park). These men got there before us and wouldn't let us get across the cattle gap. They kept us there for hours. We finally got to the boat and spent the first night of our honeymoon out in the river where the buoy is.

"The next morning we went into Chokoloskee because we needed supplies, some groceries and met Deaconess Bedell. She ordered us to spend the night at her house. You don't say *no* to Deaconess Bedell. Never - even Mr. Huntoon who was in charge of the Collier Company in the Everglades couldn't say *no*, to her, she just wouldn't accept that as an answer.

"Anyway, Deaconess Bedell's house was a little one bed room house. She strung a wire across the bedroom and put a sheet across it. She slept in one side and Bud and I slept in the other side. On the second night of our honeymoon! Yes, we were just inches, not feet, from each other.

"Then we went on. I never have been to Shark River so we were headed that way stopping at keys along the way for Bud to look at Indian mounds. We stopped at Duck Rock and went ashore there. I never knew where I was when he was looking for Indian Mounds. Then we got back on the route for Shark River. A terrible storm blew up, not life threatening, but a lot of wind. We came back to the clam boat that was digging clams for the Marco Clam Factory, where Bud would be working.

"When we got married, Bud resigned his job as postmaster for Collier City North and Collier City South and took a job as manager of the Doxsee Clam Factory because it paid $35.00 a week and that was more money than he was making at the post office. So, we got to the clam dredge and the mess hall was on the second floor of the dredge. There was a big long dining hall with a long table. The table still had food on it from their lunch, cold macaroni and cheese, and bacon covered with the oil that it was cooked with. Somehow inside that boat, I took one look at the table and headed for the upper railing for the side of the boat. As long as we were down in the little boat, with the spray hitting my face, I was fine. I was having a great time. But, in that dredge I got sea sick, I couldn't even go back home in Bud's boat. I came back in the clam boat and was sick all the way to the dock. When I put my feet on firm ground I was well."

One day while visiting Kappy's home I picked up a little carving of a water animal made from a tusk. She told me that Deaconess Bedell gave it to her. The carving had an amazing story.

Deaconess Bedell's story as told to Kappy: "I was attending a lecture and they were talking about the Indians in Canada way in the backcountry. There was no one there to talk to them and teach them. I applied for the job. They said they didn't have any money to send a person up there. I said 'I have my retirement money, I'll use that.'

"So I had not been in this snow covered area long when a man came down on a bobsled and said his wife was dying and she needed a doctor.

"I said, 'I'm not a doctor, but I will go and see what I can do for her.' The woman was very sick. I didn't have anything but a little bottle of iodine with me. I took a glass of water and put one or two drops of iodine in it and gave it to the woman. The lady got better. Her husband gave me the little carving."

After hearing this story from Kappy I asked her why the Deaconess gave her this carving?

Kappy just smiled and said it was a thank you gift, "We were very close I helped her with her Sunday school class and worked with her in Caxambas, when I was younger before I got married. I went with her to her meetings, driving everywhere. She never drove over 30 miles an hour. I used to go almost crazy driving with her. I would take her in my car, because she wouldn't let anyone drive her car. She put on her Christmas programs, anything she did like that I helped her with. She was sure she was going to make an Episcopalian out of me. She kept on at Bud so much, Bud was staying at the Lodge at that time he was fishing and guiding. Finally, Bud said, 'Deaconess Bedell, I love you very much, but I can tell you right now, I was born a Catholic, raised a Catholic and I will die a Catholic and I am not going to be an Episcopalian. She said, 'Bud, we understand each other' and she never badgered him anymore about being and Episcopalian.' But she thought surely she was going to make one out of me."

"Did she go to any place besides Marco, Immokalee?"

"Mostly she went to Everglades and out in the woods with the Indians. She went to Caxambas, she didn't go to Marco. They bought the mission house when they bought all the other houses, but a hurricane destroyed it."

"That is where she would teach Sunday school and sewing classes?"

"She had a little sleeping area there also, so she could spend the night."

"I have heard that she taught the Indians how to drive her car and that is how she became friendly with the Indians, they would drive her car".

"She might have taught them to drive, but she wouldn't let anyone drive her car. She drove herself. Maybe out in the woods, she let them drive.

"They would take her by boat or by car?"

"Yes."

Kappy explained to me how she and Bud became garbage collectors, "After I sold the store to Elva, I ran the post office; the fish house, and the garbage business. We needed someone to collect garbage. Bud had lots of friends from Rochester, where he grew up, who would come down to fish. One of them was in the garbage business in Rochester.

"One day he said, 'Bud that is a good business, why don't you get into it?' Bud thought he might give it a try.

"The friend loaned Bud two or three thousand dollars, whatever he needed, to buy the truck, Tommie Dee drove the garbage truck for two years. When she was in high school one time a pickup truck is all we had, because a man had wrecked our car. She didn't want to ride in that pickup truck, if she had to ride in it, she'd get out and walk two or three blocks to school She didn't want to be caught in that pickup truck. But, she loved the garbage truck, she loved it and drove it for two years. We served the whole island with that truck, and took the trash to the garbage disposal. They had a place on Marco where they loaded it and hauled it up to Naples. The county worked against us as hard as they could. The garbage business turned out to be a lucrative thing, the County wanted to get people to pay them. Mr. Pistor is one who worked very hard against us, to get us out of business. They really hassled us. We had a thing on the back of the truck that opened up and the garbage went in it. The whole seal went all the way around it. The seal was kind of broken at the top, about six inches. Nothing would ever have gone all the way to the top. If it got 2/3 full that was as much as we could carry. They (the county) would pull us over and every so often we'd have to take the truck in and get it fixed. Every time they found something wrong with it they would pull us over. We only had one truck. While the truck was being repaired, we didn't have a garbage truck. One time one of the lights didn't work, they pulled us over for that reason. The garbage never used the lights because it was always picked up in daytime. But they pulled us over anyway.

"After being pulled over ten times, a friend of ours said, 'Bud I'm going to get that truck fixed.'

"Bud replied, 'Now, I can't keep them off of my back.'

"The friend lived up Highway 41 area. He said, 'I'll take that truck up to my cousin who has a shop. He'll get it in tiptop shape. I'll bring it back down and you won't have any more trouble with it.'

"So he took it up at night, he used the back roads so no one would see it. He got it fixed up and inspected. He brought it back after dark. The next day the state man was down here to check the truck and they couldn't find anything wrong with it. No one ever reported anything after that. There was never anything really wrong with it, just a little light here or there that didn't work. We sold the business. The garbage people that have the service now wanted it real bad, but Bud didn't want to sell it to those people. He sold it to another man and finally that man sold it to them anyway.

"I handled the business end of it, billing and collecting money and he did the pickup from house to house, just as it is done now. Later we had a girl that handled the billing end of it."

The Goodland Bridge

"During the Depression a man was building the Goodland Bridge and he needed someone to do the survey work. He asked Bud if he would do it. Bud said he didn't know anything about survey work but the man agreed to show him. He worked at that helping to build that bridge."

"Twice I taught school the Scripp School in Caxambas. The First and Second grades were in one room, Third and Fourth in another downstairs. Left hand-side upstairs were Sixth, Seventh, and Eight and the Juniors and Seniors were in the other side. They had four teachers. Each teacher taught several grades.

"Kare was four when I was teaching the second time. I took her to school with me and she sat in the back of the room and colored. Mrs. Florence from Naples was in charge as the overseer of the school. She was in my classroom observing my class when I was talking to the first or second grade. A child could not answer a question and Kare piped up, 'Oh, you know the answer to that J__. It is so and so.' Mrs. Florence looked at me and said, 'Kappy that child needs to be in school, even though she was only four years old.' The next year she went in the Second Grade, and did the Second Grade and Third Grade in one year.

That may have started something because when little Faye Weeks begged her mother to let her go to school with her big sister Annette, her mother finally said, "Well come and get dressed, if Kare can go to school at four you can go to school at five." Faye said, "Mama didn't waste any time driving over the sand hills. When we started climbing the long flight of steps to the second floor of the school building, I clung on tightly to mama's hand. We walked into the class room where Mr. Heath, the principle, was teaching the high school children. He looked up from behind his desk and said, "Vergie, what can I do for you?" That was all he said and the next thing I knew, Mrs. Otter had me signed into school and asked Jimmy Lowe to take me up to the black board and teach me my numbers to one hundred. Jimmy and I were neighbors and good buddies. I caught on fast and made top grades in Mrs. Otter's class, grades one through three."

Kappy with Hound Dogs and Roy Roberts holding Kare

Kappy talked about Bud's hound dogs, he had 14 of them. They fed them from meal and stuff from the store and cooked it in the water bucket. Sometimes, Bud would bring fish for them. Kappy got tired of it and said, "Bud, some of these dogs go or I go." He agreed. The only one they kept was the mean old hound dog.

Kappy said, "He'd let Kare wallow all over him, but he wouldn't let anyone else touch him."

"Did you keep him for hunting?"

"He was a hunting dog, but I don't think Bud took him hunting."

"So, you had 14 dogs and they didn't go hunting?"

"That is right, I just fed them."

Trying to understand I asked, "Bud loved them? The children loved them? You just ended up with them?"

She answered, "I guess Bud was going to go hunting. Those were puppies that they were going to raise as hunting dogs, but it didn't happen, one of those good ideas that is never followed up on."

Fish House

"When we first came over here, the property where the Lodge is now was owned by a man named Bob Combs, who owned the Combs Fish

Company in Naples years and years ago. Bud leased the property from him to run a Fish House on it. He was only there a short time when Bob sold the property to Rex Johnson. So we were out of the fish business for awhile. In 1964 we built this fish house that was the second time. We built one before and called it The Fishing Well. Then we added to it. I think in 1964 we built this last one. Bud would manage the fish house most of the time, but later on Damos took it over, and other people would manage it. Bud would stand it as long as he could then he would have to go fishing."

Houses from Marco

As you drive into Goodland the road turns right just as you come to Stans Idle Hour restaurant. There are little cottages that had been moved from the village of Marco.

Kappy explained, "The houses from Marco were little row houses like the ones in Caxambas, built around 1910 for people to live in who worked at the Doxsee Clam Factory in Marco. I don't think Doxsee actually built them, I think the Captain Bill Collier built them. The same thing happened in Caxambas six years earlier. Uncle Jim built all those houses along there for the married men who worked at Burnham Clam Factory. He built the Stephens Hotel that Grandmother ran for the single men. They rented the cottages to the workers with families. When the Company was getting ready for the Marco Development, they brought them to Goodland to clear them off the land at Caxambas. Mr. Joe Douglas, a retired Chevrolet engineer and his wife Ivy are living in one of those that was bought over. It wasn't on cinder blocks, as it is now. It was on pillars. Ellen Bradley's husband bought the one next to it. The last one on the end of the street belongs to Stan Gober. He is living in a house built in 1939 that was brought over. Stan's music festivals on the weekend and his annual Mullet Festival with a contest for the best costume and dancer of the Buzzard Lope became famous."

CHAPTER 7

William and Marie Ludlow

Kappy and I drove from Marco Island to Fort Myers during a rain storm one Thursday afternoon, August 2, 2001 to visit Bill and Marie Ludlow. They welcomed us and had the table spread with pictures for us to go through.

They also had an old fashioned lighted picto-scope. When I looked inside it I was suddenly transported to a meeting at the old Scripp School house where all the villagers were gathered, sitting at student desks with their children. I believe they were listening to Deaconess Bedell at the front of the room. I will never forget that experience, it was like traveling back in time to the era I longed to learn about.

Marie and Bill lived in Caxambas as newlyweds one year before the move to Goodland. After the move, they lived in Goodland for the next twenty years before following Bill's job to Fort Myers.

Marie had not lived in Goodland for over thirty years but she was able to recall names, places, people, incidents, as though it was only yesterday. Bill often came up with the names or words that she couldn't think of at the moment. In one afternoon, we mapped out the entire village of Goodland because of her incredible memory.

Edward, Marie, Rufus and Beverly at the orphanage

Marie was the daughter of Hilburn Smith born in Everglades. Her father eventually moved to Marco, where he guided for the Inn. After Marie's mother died she and her siblings ended up in the orphanage while her Dad went off with his pregnant girlfriend to live in a *poor do*, so poor he couldn't do anything else. She explained to me how she got out of the orphanage with the help of her uncle who brought her back to Marco. Marie lived in the barracks at Marco until she could bring out her two brothers Edward and Rufus, and sister Beverly. She was working for Elva Griffis at the G and G Mercantile store when she met William Ludlow.

It's a great story that I included in *Island Voices* published in 2006.

Marie Smith

With pride in her voice Marie said for my benefit, "William, son of John Ludlow, grandson of Frederick Ludlow, one of 'the first families' living in Caxambas the other end of the Island."

William was quick to point out that he was actually not born there, because his mother went to Ocala to have her baby, but he had lived there since infancy.

At this point the tape in my recorder needed to be flipped and by the time I was able to get it in operation the topic had changed to the old Army Barracks from Marco Point.

Marie was saying, "During the war the army had built a barrack on the northwest point of Marco by the G & G Mercantile store. It was on the waterfront and had a good dock."

Bill pointed out that the army used good wood to build the barrack and dock and it was still quite good. Marie nodded and continued, "The new owners of the property in Marco had purchased it from Captain Bill Collier and had plans for the northwest point. He was going to build up the dock for his use, but they didn't want the building. The barrack was given to my Daddy, Hilburn Smith."

Marie went on with barely a pause in her monologue, "The hotel wanted the old army building off the land. This man who managed the property, I can't think of his name, wanted it gone. "What was the name of that man?" she asked William. He supplied the name the Ruppert.

"It was a beautiful point, I don't know what they were going to do with it, but I guess they felt that it would look better with that barrack off. They had plans to use the build up and use the dock. My Daddy, Captain Hilburn Smith, was guiding for the hotel, so they gave it to him.

"But the man said Daddy would have to move it. Daddy made a deal with Bill Haney and he said that the way he would get the money to move it was that he would take it, saw it in half, he would give Hilburn one half and he would sell 1/4 to J.P. Robinson and his brother Herbert Robinson. Bill Haney moved the Robinson's half over to Caxambas, where the two houses remained until the buildings were moved to Goodland. Daisy Walker ended up with one of them."

Marie pointed out, "William and I got all the lumber out of our part. We tore it down to start our house in Goodland. First, however we took all the lumber to Caxambas to store under Kappy and Bud's house, then when they moved, we had to move the lumber. "We moved it over to his Daddy's house, then we moved it to Goodland."

"We moved that lumber a dozen times," Bill declared.

"It was in about a year and a half that we did all that," Marie nodded.

William Ludlow

Bill continued the story, "When the lumber was stored under Kappy's house, Bud had some old hounds that slept under there. They had fleas. Then the dogs had puppies and the puppies had fleas. When I went under there to pull the wood out," Bill said, "I was black with fleas. They just eat me up. When I got home, I just stripped my clothes off there on the porch."

Marie laughed, "That was so funny, seeing him come into the house like that." Marie said, "Well my goodness we don't all have that much modesty."

"Well, I didn't want to bring in the fleas," he explained.

"Where were you living at the time?" I asked.

"We were living in a chicken house," Bill replied, "rather in my Dad's coon house in Caxambas. He had a coon house and a chicken house."

William and sister Kathleen in front of the "coon house" next to the big house

"Did you say coon house?" I asked thinking I might have heard him wrong.

He replied, "Years and years ago when out fishing, my Dad used to coon hunt a lot. They'd just count tails. You know in 1929 that was a lot of money. My Dad used to kill all of them. Then he began raising coons. He had nine to ten in a house. The coon house had wood shutters on it to let down in case of rain. When Marie and I got married, we white-washed it inside, cleaned it up good, put screens on the windows, then put a chest-of-drawers in there, a bed, a little sink."

"We had a small table and my stove from the barrack in Marco," added Marie

"We had a baby crib in there. We had Glenda," said Bill.

"No! We didn't take the crib in there!" she protested.

"I believe we did."

"No, Your *Mother* wanted us to move into her house, she tried to shame us because we wanted to put our baby in a coon house. Your Mother said, 'I have a bedroom here in the big house and there is no sense in it. Furthermore, that is an old damp building that doesn't even have good windows. You have to run outside to lower them when it rains.'

"We did have to let down the shutters," Marie said for my information, "you couldn't even do that from the inside. Mrs. Ludlow said, 'I would be ashamed. There is a bedroom in there.'"

"So that is when we got her crib. We had room for the crib in the big house. So, we were living with Mamma and Daddy in 1949 when the Goodland move began."

Bill scratched his head, "I remember when Daddy's house was moved to Goodland we went with them. The big house is still in Goodland, on Goodland Drive East, Steve Camacho owns it now," he added.

Bill and Marie Ludlow home in Goodland

"Let me tell you how we got started when our house was built," Bill said turning to me, because Kappy had heard all this before. "We put the foundation down. We got the walls up and we got the roof up. But, the way we did it was slow. We were all commercial fishermen, then. If we made a hundred dollars, or fifty dollars, we'd go buy a window. Ten dollars would buy a window then. Or we'd buy one or two boards at a time. Good boards. The main frame was made of good wood.

"We bought an old house from Pat Leo. It was the old power plant they used to provide electricity for Caxambas. When they tore that down we used some of that lumber.

"On the inside of the house we just floored half of the house. Do you remember that the old power plant was a tin building? He said glancing toward Kappy who nodded yes. Old corrugated tin. We took the old corrugated tin and partitioned half of the house with it. Up in the attic we put cheesecloth." To me he said, "You know what cheese cloth is? " I nodded yes, and he said, "We put cheesecloth to keep the mosquitoes out. We lived in two bedrooms for a long time like that. We had a shower from the artesian well. The Collier Company drilled an artesian well over there on the point. "

Bill turned to his wife and Kappy who were having their own conversation and asked, "It is still there isn't it Kappy, that old well by your place? At the old Stickle place?"

"No, I don't think it is," Kappy answered.

"That was an artesian well and they ran a pipe for the artesian well to some of the houses to get water to them. Well, we ran a hose up in the rafters, of the building, one quarter of the building, that was our shower!"

"An indoor shower," I said thinking about trying to shower with cold water from a hose.

"Yes," he said with a certain amount of pride, "We had some chickens roosting in one quarter of the building. They didn't belong to us, they were just roosting there. Who did those chickens belong to Marie? Frederick and them?"

"They were ours," she answered.

"Okay, they were ours, I thought they were someone else's."

William Ludlow and Glenda

Marie replied, "Don't you remember that Glenda had named one of them Sampson? And we asked H. L. to go in to get chickens because we were going to get rid of 'em. To kill 'em and eat 'em. Don't you remember? Glenda got hold of H. L. and said, 'You turn my chicken loose.' She was just beating on the poor guy."

"Then, after we cooked him Marie said, 'Do you know what chicken that is?'"

"No, I didn't say that, protested Marie. "Mother Ludlow said that. I wouldn't have been that cruel."

"Well, after Glenda had eaten a piece of it, she *was told*, 'that is Sampson,' and Glenda just said, 'Give me another piece, Daddy," Bill chortled.

"…and that just tickled me to death, because that didn't rile her any," Marie smiled at the memory.

"Then, after that house got up, we lived in it. We put in a window here and a window there. Then we started on our cistern. You know what a cistern is Betsy?"

"Yes, it is a water tank in the ground that holds rainwater."

"We had two of them in the back of the building."

"Wait," I said, "So, even though you had the artesian well from the Collier Company you still had to have a cistern?"

"Oh, we couldn't drink the well water. You could only wash in it. We had to catch rainwater to drink.

"After we got the house kind of half way fixed we had to dig a cistern. The way we did it, we didn't have a drag line or anything. We couldn't afford to have a dragline to come in and dig it out. No one to help us, it was just Marie and me."

"It was just pure shell wasn't it? How did you get it out?"

"I had an old '36 Buick," Bill responded proud of his resourcefulness, "that I had wrecked going over towards Caxambas, you know the high hills? I hit a fish truck one night getting ready to go fishing and smack, I wrecked it. I went to an old junkyard to find a wheel to put on it. So, we used it. We had an old scoop that came out of the clam factory in Caxambas. A shell scoop, do you know what that looked like? It looked like a wheel barrel. We would dig the rim into the shells out like this and then scoop them up. Marie and I would get out there after dinner, around night time. She'd dig the scoop down into the shell and I'd take the old Buick and pull it up and then she'd dump it. I got an old cement mixer from Roy Rimes who lived at Marco. The bottom was all rusted out, so I covered it all with chicken wire and then cemented it. It worked good! After that fell off I put some metal around it. But, anyway, we took footboards, made our frame for the cement cistern. We'd pour that a little bit, put steel in it, when that would cure hard, we'd pull it up, put the pin back in the board, put a small wire with steel in it and go on up. How far did we go up, Marie, eight feet?"

"One end of it was eight feet the other end was seven feet. We built it on a slant. There were two of them built the same way. At the end of rainy season we put all our water in one cistern…" Bill added, "and we'd wash the other out, clean it out," The way we did it was that we slanted the floor a little bit, just like a pool, so that the water would run down into a little basin. You could pump it out and get rid of ever-bit of it. There wasn't anything that was in there and you'd wash it down with Clorox. We built the first one and Carl Salo built the second one.

"The old lumber we took out of it we built a little apartment over the cisterns. Later we built a carport, 60 feet long, forty feet wide?"

"No, 48 feet long, 20 feet wide, then we put another apartment in there, there were three apartments in that house."

"You rented them out?"

"Yes, but we didn't do that until Glenda left home. We just kept building on our own."

"We rented it for $125.00 a month."

"How did you keep the water fresh? I've always wondered?"

"All that bird stuff in the cistern? That made it good!" Bill said with a laugh.

"The funniest thing happened to us when we sold the home to Lucretia," Marie said looking over at Kappy to get her attention, "I don't believe I've ever told you this story. When she wanted to buy our house, she said, 'Well, I've run into another problem.'"

"I asked her, 'and what is that? I told you that you could buy this house. I will sell it to you for this amount but I don't want to hear any griping about that house.' We told her that it had termites in it, and that it had one little place that might leak. I told her that I was going to give her a thousand dollars for the roof, back then that would have done the whole roof."

Marie continued, "But I don't want to hear one complaint about the house. If there is something you don't like about the house, just fix it and keep your mouth shut."

"Lucretia said, 'Oh, you won't hear anything from me.' So I get a phone call from her. She says, 'I got a problem.'"

"I told her to keep it to herself."

"She said, 'No, I think you can help me out with this. I have to have it before I can buy this, before they will finalize the papers, I have to have a water check done on the water in the cistern. To send in a sample to see what is in the water.'"

"I told her, 'Well you've got everything…we've been drinking that for years and none of us are dead yet'."

"Lucretia said, 'No, but the government has a funny way of doing things.' So probably two weeks later, she came up to get a refrigerator that we gave her."

"She told us, 'Well the check came back. They said they couldn't find anything in the water. But, I am going to have to put a purifier on it.'"

"Oh for goodness sake you're kidding."

"'Nope, they say I have to have a purifier. Can you understand why they say I have to put a purifier on rainwater?'"

"No, but if you want to get the papers signed then you'd better do it. She said, 'We have a good freshet pump set up on it perfect, and they had to take it all apart and put a purifier on it.'"

At this point I asked her a question, "That was back in 1971. Are most of those houses over there still using cisterns?"

"Oh, yes. I guess if I had been living there when they forced the people to use the main water supply, I still wouldn't use it. There is nothing better to use than rainwater to wash your hair, take a bath. It makes white clothes, so white."

Moving the "Big House"

"The Colliers' had three men come over. I have pictures later on I'll show you. Two of them were black people. We didn't have black people in Caxambas. A lot of people would come down and watch them work. Mr. Ludlow's house was among the first ones, but it was not the first one."

"What did they do to move a house?" I asked.

"They jacked it up and put the dollies under it. The dollies look like great big piling things with wheels. They'd jack up the house and then run the truck back with the dollies and then let the house back down on the dollies. Then they took the house right on over, no problem at all. I don't, think they had a problem with any house did they?" Marie asked looking at Kappy.

"They did with the store," she replied. "They had to cut it in two."

"What about the plumbing?" I asked. "Did they have to disconnect the plumbing and electricity?"

"Well, there wasn't a lot of plumbing," they all laughed.

"The water all came from Pat Leo's well," Kappy explained.

"You used out houses in Caxambas?"

"Some of them down the other way did. But, Kappy's didn't. I think it just emptied back down into the bay didn't it?" asked Marie mischievously looking at Kappy.

"Old piping down into the bay," was her short reply, meaning that the tide flushed it away. I guessed this was a touchy topic with some people.

"The Pettits' did too. I know that all down on that side did. I don't know what the rest used down the other way."

"I had to take Glenda down to Kappy's store," to use the bathroom.

Bill added, "Some of them had an old barrel in the ground down in the swamp: the old sewer went down into there. It would get stopped up and you'd go down and dig everything out."

"What a job that must have been," I said and my tape cassette needed to be flipped.

Chapter 8
Marie maps out Goodland

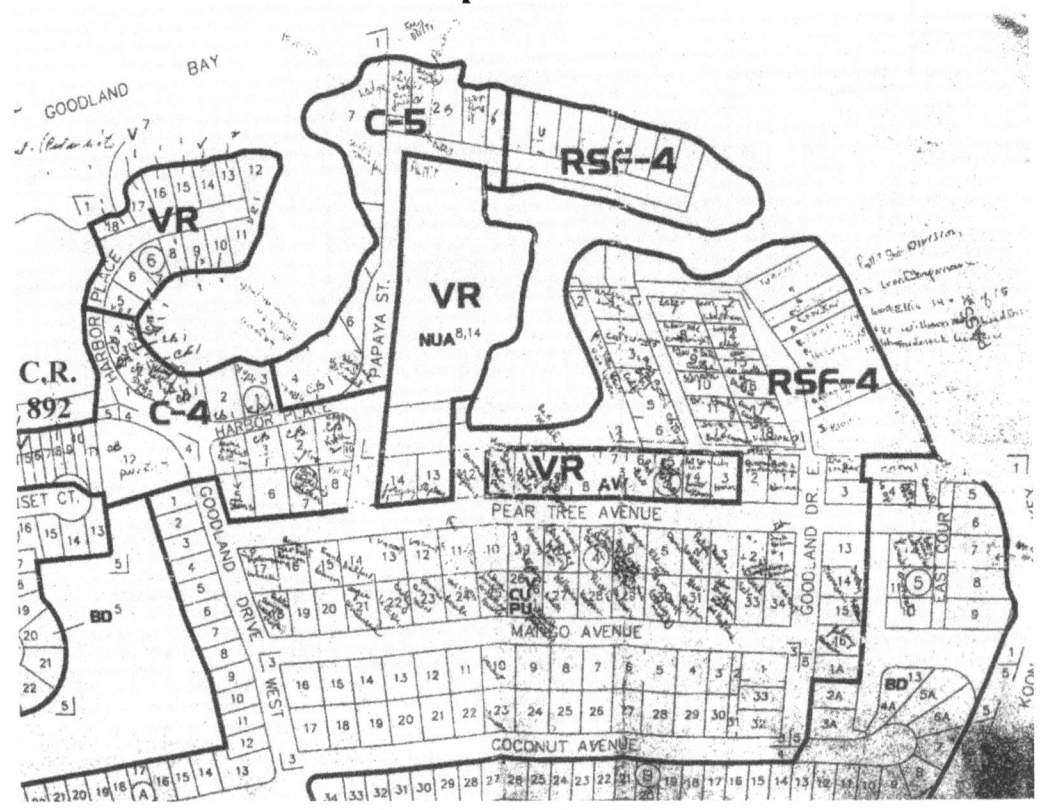

Goodland Plat Map

"What fish house are we talking about?" I asked, trying to catch up with all the conversations going on.

"This is the *Key Hole* (C5 on the plat map) see how Papaya Street runs right into it. It is not there now," she said pointing to the top of the Goodland Plat.

Kappy elaborated, "You know Betsy, where Little Bar restaurant is down around the corner past our fish house… where the Lodge is now."

"No Kappy," Marie corrected, "the Lodge is on the place where the other fish house was that Hamp Bagley had. That was out here. But the Key Hole was here, straight down from the post office. Hamp Bagley was next to Fred Waggoner's house. He was out on the water on stilts. He had a little old thing like a Poor Do, it was a little on shacky looking thing they lived in down at the camp. They brought that over from Caxambas. Then he had pilings put in and they built his house out on the water. He had a ramp. Well he lived in that little Poor Do about the size of a ten by twelve room."

"Next to that was the Stone Crab. They had bought this piece of property, I believe there is a restaurant there now, haven't been there in years."

Marie called over to Kappy who was looking through some pictures with Bill. "Kappy, what was the name of the lady that was the sister of the cop's father-in-law? Remember she gave us that furniture? She lived out on the waterfront?"

Kappy came up with the name Yourstone for Marie.

"No, not Yourstone that was her lot and the Yourstone's was right there. Beyond that I wasn't there. My house was right here," Marie pointed out the third lot on Goodland Drive East toward the water.

"We used to go down to that man's property. We could see straight down to the fish house. That was a piece. This canal didn't go through to the little basin. They must have dug this barrier out after we left."

"Is that why they called that a basin?"

"Yes, it wasn't a bay then. There was no outlet. That basin was made when they scraped the shells out to make the airport in Naples. Everybody that lived on this street was supposed to have rights down here on the water, but it didn't happen."

"Do you mean the right to dock your boat?" I asked.

"Yes. Chapman had a dock and so did Lehr's. They owned this property here too, but they sold it to Cartwrights.

"Then from there all this was Mar Good cottages. Back of Mar Good's is Jane and Babo Camacho. That is Stevie Camacho's mother and daddy's house, next to that is an empty lot."

I understood the people she was referring to were Captain Bill and Emma Ludlow Collier's daughter Jane and grandchild Steve Camacho whom I met much earlier. He told me that he had his grandfather's watch. He promised to bring it to a reception at the Collier County museum. I was so disappointed when he didn't bring it. His excuse that it was being repaired made me wonder if he even had it.

Marie continued, "Then there is George and Betty Culpe. Next to the Culpes' were people from Minnesota called Gran. Next to Grans' was Doctor Pauley."

"Goodness, you are really good at remembering this," I said, awed at her capacity to recall these details.

"No, I'm not really," Marie laughed. She was pleased but on a roll, "Now, across the street if you follow me, were these cottages Mar Good cottage. Cartwrights owned this before they bought the other. These people were from Miami and their names were…what was Andrew Anderson's brother's name?" she asked her husband or Kappy. "They bought down on the water by Lehr's and had a moving company in Miami? He had two pieces of property really. This is where they built right out on the water."

No one could help her out or come up with the name, so she continued on.

"Ruby and Rex Johnson wanted to buy this piece of property, I don't know if they ever did. When we left in '71, she came over to me and wanted me to go talk her into selling it to them. I said I couldn't do that."

"Why did you move away Marie?"

"Bill had a job north of Fort Myers. He was going back and forth all the time. He was helping build *Burnt Store* over at Cape Coral. I was really worried about him. You could set a clock by him actually. But, if he was a little late, I'd panic."

"Oh, I see," I said nodding my head.

"Harry Pettit owned all of this land," she said looking at the plat map. He subdivided it and lived in a house on Papaya. Then he lived in another one. He had a house here, and Curley Shaeffer had a house there. They must have divided it because it was directly opposite. The Poor Do was here. Grandmother stayed in that one."

"What was the man's name that you could smell him coming, Kappy?"

"We called him Stinky," she answered causing Marie to grin.

"Later he stayed down in there. Kappy's store was directly across from her house. I have a picture of that with the nets all spread. Before your fish house was there."

"Johnny Stephen's house was katty-corner from here; he is Tommie Barfield's brother. Johnny Morrison lived here back then. Bill, your sister Kathleen Ludlow Pattison owned this one right here and they sold it to Billy. Dorothy and Nanny (Emma Collier) own this one. She had that beautiful trailer brought in. Then she gave it to her son Babo and he sold it. He could have rented it out. It was a new trailer, she drew her own plans and had that built, it was beautiful.

"Dorothy Thomason owned it, not Ed Thomason. She moved out of Nanny's and into a trailer. I don't remember who she sold it to, was it Billy and Virginia?" Bill asked.

Kappy said, "Dorothy was staying there. Who owned the lot on the corner? I thought two of them bought side by side and had a house almost exactly alike?"

"They did, Kappy," Marie continued, "Kathleen bought over here by Morrisons' and built. They built somewhere by the Marshes then they moved from there and built a big place where they are now."

"I thought their first place was by Coon Key Cottages," Kappy added.

"They did own Coon Key Cottages. Then they built out on the water, and then they sold that and moved to the place where they are now.

"This was Neeses", she said pointing to a lot on Pear Tree Avenue. This was Doris Ellison's. This was also Doris Ellison's and she built a motel on it.

"Kappy do you remember the man who was head of the Boy Scouts?"

"Ivan…?"

"Ivan Burleigh, that's it. The choir director had a trailer here on Pear Tree Avenue. I can't remember that man's name.

"When daddy lived there this lot was vacant for a long time, but Ruby and Rex Johnson bought it and they put two of those little houses from Marco on it. Later, Cecilia and Ralph Weeks lived there in back of George. Here is Shirley Stephens' across the street and Johnny Stephens is right there, right across the street from the Post Office. He has two little houses going one way and one going the other way. This was America's Stephens. The trailer park was Rex Johnson's. Rex's show building was the big cement building that is now Mar Good."

"George Griffin."

"Old man Johnny Stephens owned this one. This was the one that was vacant and Little Johnny Stephens wanted to buy. He did, his son bought it, not Larry but Terry.

"This was Bickerds he owned these two little lots, katty-corner from Kappy."

Kappy said, "Ray Bisichnich bought those two. They came down from Indiana and bought Clara Mae Rawl's house."

"Oh, I didn't know them."

"This would have been Johnny Stephens' lot, he has two going this way and one going this way. Then there is the other Stephens. This would be part of the old Rex Johnson's trailer park and then the big show building would be in this one that became Mar Good. I don't know what they did with the show building. On this side is Rex's motel."

"Old man Johnson and America Stephens. Mary's, Nanny's and Lorries. Hank Keene's later on but it was Lily Hanes then. This would have been Pat Leo's. Rex Johnson had another lot right here, by the show building, going up to his place.

"This was Rex's trailer park, not the big one that is over there now. But, I believe, that Rex moved some trailers that were over at Caxambas on it.

"Here is Bob and Mary, our house, Pat Leo, then Mar Good."

William said, "Mar Good's was Rex's. He built it to store his old cars. He used to have these little cars to run around the block: he would charge a dime a piece to run around the block, past the Cash and Carry, the old store from Caxambas. He used that old building to store his cars in. He stored old out board motors, anything. He'd go north and lock them up."

"The cottages that were back of our house, one was Betty Culpe's house right in here. That was Rex's mother that bought it. They were from Kelly Gant's fish house on Marco, a real good friend. He put three of them, two on this lot and one back of Betty Culpe's. I used to work for him over at Marco, close to Elva's place the G & G."

"Did they have to clear it off like the G & G?"

"I don't think they had to move them, I think Kelly Gant built some new houses, didn't he?"

"I don't remember," Kappy said with a tired smile.

We were all exhausted but now had a pretty complete picture of early Goodland, who lived where, the commercial lots and the empty lots after the move.

HARBOR PLACE

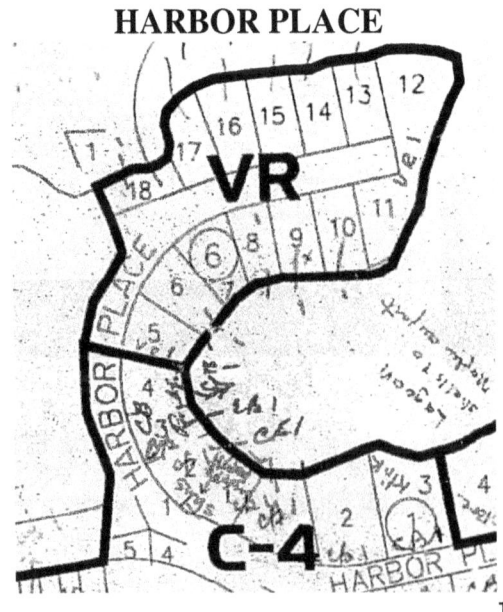

1. Commercial   Kirk
2. Commercial   Kirk
3. Commercial
4. Commercial
1 - 2 Herbert Robinson/Stan Gober
  "Stan's Idle Hour" and
  commercial parking
3 – 4 Commercial
5 – 18 Unknown

PAPAYA

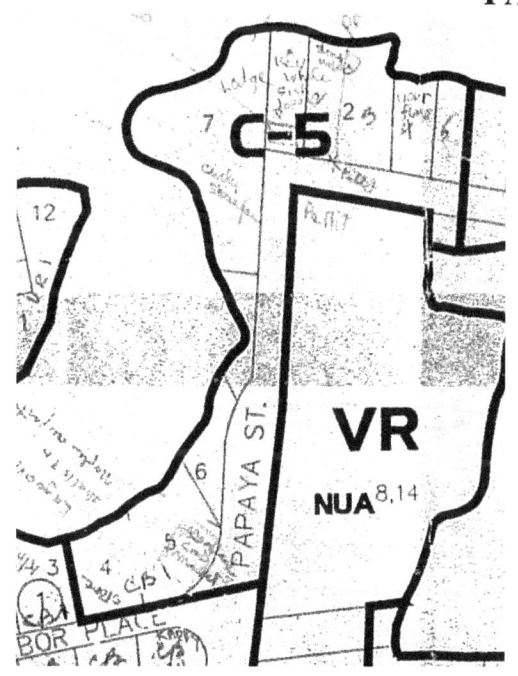

4. Store
5. Goodland Cash and Carry (On corner Harbor Pl. & Papaya)
6. Unknown
7. Curley Shafer/Lodge
7. Fred Wagner stilt house on water - Goodland Bay
1. Key Hole Fish House on water
2. Stone crab - Goodland Bay
2. Pettit's
3. Stone crab parking - across from *poor do* - Goodland Bay
4. Yourstone Goodland Bay
5. Unknown Goodland Bay

GOODLAND DRIVE WEST

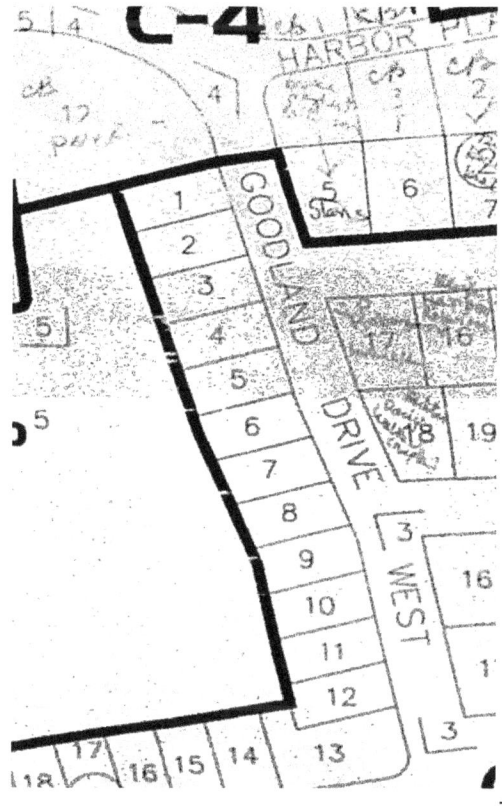

1 – 13 Goodland Drive West, west side unknown
4 - 5. North corner of Pear Tree Bessie Herbert Robinson, later Stan Gober (Stan's)
17   South corner of Pear Tree J. P. Robinson
18. North corner Mango Avenue Fulton Daisy Walker (Naples)

GOODLAND DRIVE EAST (Northern Portion)

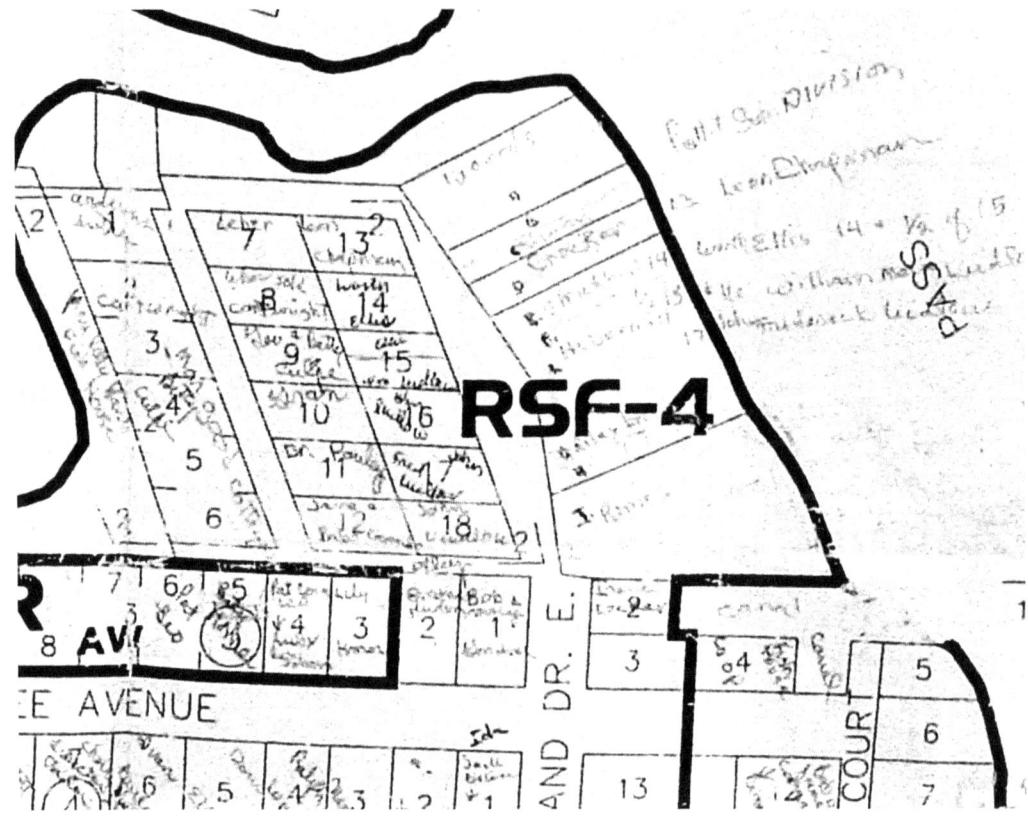

Left to right

1. Anderson brothers
7. Leher
2 Cartwright
8 Cartwright
3 Mar Good Cottages
9 Geo & Betty Culpe
4 Mar Good Cottages
4 Geo & Betty Culpe
10 Gran
5 Mar Good Cottages
11 Dr. Pauley
6. Mar Good Cottages
12 Jane, Babo Camacho
Kelly Gantt Fish House
Kelly Gantt Fish House
21 Anne Bianchi

Left to right

13. Leon Chapman
A. Woods
14 Worth Ellis
B. Unknown
C. Grahn
15 ½ Ellis, ½ W. Ludlow
D. Crocker
16 Wm. Marie Ludlow
E. Strickland
7 Frederick Ludlow
F. Habermill
18 John Ludlow
G. Riley Brothers
1 Bob, Mary Gardner
H. Unknown

GOODLAND DRIVE EAST (Southern Portion) & EAST COURT

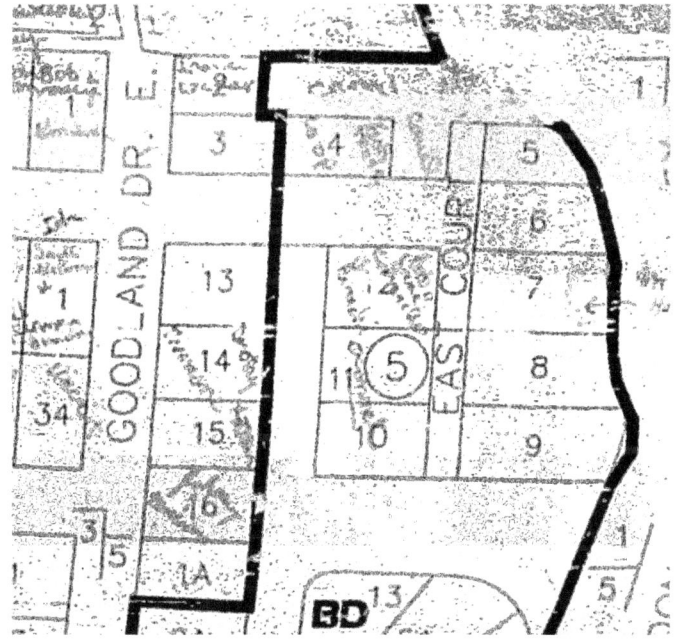

EAST COURT
4 Co-op Fish House Canal
5 unknown
6 unknown
12 Babo Jane Camacho/Bianchi
7 Macbeth Johnson houseboat
11 O'Connel
8 unknown
Coon Key Pass   10 O'Connel
9 unknown

GOODLAND DR. EAST (SO. PART)
2. Irene Locker
3. Unknown
13. Unknown
14. Dorothy Thomason
15. Kathleen Pattison
16. Johnny Morrison
1A. Unknown

PEAR TREE AVENUE
North Side of street – Left to right

5 Bessie, Herbert Robinson	12 America Stephens	5 Betsy Homer
6 unknown	11 Rex Ruby Johnson Trailer Park	4 Pat, Cora Leo/Rex, Ruby Johnson
7 Turk Dickerson's brother	10 Mar Good Bldg	
8 Kirk	9 Rex Johnson Motel	3 Lily Homer
1 unknown	8 unknown	2 Emma Hudson
14 Johnny Stephens (Ludlow) Gardner	7 unknown	1 Bob, Mary
13 Johnny Stephens	6 Pat & Cora Leo	

South Side of street – Left to right

17 J. P. Robinson	11 Unknown	5 Doris Ellison
16 Bessie, Herbert Robinson	10 Unknown	4 Ralph Weeks
15 Frank Robinson	9 Vacant later/Terry Stephens	3 Neese
14 Bickford	8 Vacant/Rex, Ruby Johnson	2 Russell Blimpke
13 Vacant	7 Choir Director trailer	1 Jack Bower/Anna Bianchi (310)
12 Vacant	6 Ivan Burleigh/Wardell & Sarah Weeks	

MANGO AVENUE
North Side of street – Left to right

18 Fulton Daisy Walker (Naples)	24 George & Cecelia Rawls	30 Vacant/Ellison Motel
19 X	25 Clara Mae, Brownie Rawls	31 George Griffin
20 X	26 Church Property	32 George Griffin (mother married Kirkland)
21 Angie Wiesenreid	27 Hilburn Smith	
22 Bradley Weeks	28 Rinnie brothers	33 Carl Salo
23 Tommie Dee Moss	29 Annie Anderson	34 Vacant

South Side of street – Left to right

16 unknown	10 Vacant	4 unknown
15 unknown	9 unknown	3 unknown
14 unknown	8 unknown	2 unknown
13 unknown	7 unknown	1 unknown
12 unknown	6 unknown	
11 unknown	5 unknown	

COCONUT AVE

23 Lucas

    We had done a lot of work in the short time we were there. It was fascinating to reminisce with Marie and William, but it was time to go. We folded the plat map, gathered the few pictures they were willing to loan for me to scan and return. We began saying our goodbyes.

    "Did you see this?" Bill asked. "This is a Christmas Tree angel. President Clinton wanted a Christmas tree angel for the top of the National Christmas tree. So, he asked several people to send in angels and he chose this one. The artist made three of them, she gave us one, sent one to the White House, and gave one to a friend of hers. It is made out of ceramic. The angels head was done separately and then fused to the rest."

    Kappy and I admired that and another piece the artist made and looked at the beautiful beaded glass doors and ceiling light fixtures that is a striking feature of the Ludlow's' décor.

Marie and Bill ushered us out to the car with umbrellas and invited us back to see all the pictures and talk more about how it all came about. What a wonderful afternoon.

Among other things as we were leaving I was able to hold a treasure that Bill had saved. It was piece of the old Burnham Clam Factory engine, a beautiful brass and glass part that screwed on to the top of the engine to drip fuel. I could almost visualize the piece in a little box in a future exhibit at the museum we hoped to build.

We said farewell, hoping to see them again. The rain had stopped and it promised to be a beautiful evening.

CHAPTER 9
The hermit in Bud Kirk's Back Yard

Paul Teachout's fishing boat

I've written about many hermits in my newspaper column "Days Gone By" for the Marco Island Sun Times 2003 - 2011. I published a book by hermit Al Seely entitled *The Phony Hermit* in 2010. Al spent ten years living as a hermit in the Ten Thousand Islands and wrote about his life.

I didn't know about Bud Kirk's hermit until 2021 when I was invited to a viewing of "Bud Kirk's skiff "at the museum in early March. The Naples News carried this story on March 14, 1987:

> Paul Teachout was a printer and a veteran. He became an introverted gentle, hermit living on a mud flat in the swamp when Bud came across him. He had used the skiff likely built using cypress, mahogany and red mangrove – for more than 30 years for transportation and fishing. Of his own design, he built it using almost primitive, possibly 18th century tools. Instead of using nails to hold the skiff together, Teachout laboriously whittled the boat's fastenings of wooden pegs one by one. The boat has a small live-well for storing bait and an ingenious folding seat that allows the operator to row facing forward. A bulbous midsection adds to its stability and provides flotation support needed for a boat so small.

The hermit had built the skiff by hand in 1944 or 45. It was an original design, using antique tools with added bits from the junk yard. It was a work of wooden art, each strip of wood pieced together with tiny wooden pegs. It was a small craft 11 foot long, bulbous in the middle for stability and rode low in the water. It was so constructed that he could row forward, or backward sitting on the seat over the live fish well. All he had to do was change positions and row in the opposite direction. "It was bow-faced, rowed – sail used only once"

Apparently, Bud was out in his fishing boat one day when he came across a man sheltering on a mud flat in a hollow tree. Bud convinced the hermit to come to Goodland where he could live in the shack where Bud built his crab traps. It would seem like a palace compared to this hollow tree. The hermit accepted his offer.

Paul Teachout pulled his little boat on the grass near the shack and lived there doing odd carpentering jobs until his death in 75-76. Bud remembered him as a gentle, gentle man.

Five years after the hermit's death an article appeared in the newspaper.

> Bud and Kappy Kirk took in strangers, friends and strays. The only thing Teachout left behind was his boat and Kirk refused to sell it even though he received many lucrative offers. So instead, the boat sits in the Museum of Florida History (MFH)," in Tallahassee. Bud Kirk donated the fishing boat to the museum for a planned exhibit of early transportation in Florida.

In January 2021 MFH officials contacted Austin Bell curator of the Marco Island Historical Museum, who said, "They were downsizing their warehouse and needed to dispose of Bud Kirk's boat." Austin remembered the drive back as being a white-knuckle ride both ways, because of the pandemic. He had to fly to Tallahassee wearing a double mask, then drive a big box truck slowly back to Marco a 449.6 mile drive that took well over eight hours.

He found a retired Master Boat Builder Roger Johnson who with the help of Ron Rutledge donated their time to the project of restoring the boat for display in the Marco Island Historical Museum lobby.

It is a tribute to Bud Kirk that he had the foresight and thoughtfulness to save this little masterpiece by giving it to the museum up north.

I never met Bud, but I appreciated the opportunity to know him better through his kindness, what he treasured, and what he ultimately preserved, for us to display in our own museum 75 years later.

Goodland Pioneer Honored

By MARTY BONVECHIO
Staff Writer

GOODLAND — How Bud Kirk came to own the unusual little boat that sat deteriorating in his backyard for five years is a sad story. But it will have a happy ending.

Soon that handmade skiff will be honored by being displayed at the Museum of Florida History in Tallahassee.

PAUL TEACHOUT was living in a hollow log in the swamp near Goodland when Kirk found him about 10 years ago. Kirk and his wife Kappy, long-time residents of Goodland, are known for taking in people — friends, strangers, the strays of life.

Teachout lived a hermit's life on a mud flat surrounded by mangrove trees.

But it wasn't an existence he could have survived long at, so Kirk made him come to Goodland. He offered the hermit the little shack in which Kirk built crab traps, a palace compared to Teachout's hollow log. And Teachout called it home until he died about four years later.

"He was wonderful with wood," Kirk said. He managed to do odd carpentry jobs around the little village.

But his boat was his masterpiece. The nine-foot-long skiff, made of cypress and mahogany, sat low in the water. No nails hold the boat together, instead handmade wooden pegs were used.

IT WAS THE unique design and craftsmanship of the boat that caught the eye of the state

(Please see BOAT, Page 3B)

Paul Teachout's skiff to be housed in state museum.

NAPLES Daily News MAR 14 1987

Boat

From Page 1B

museum. Tom Baker, a museum spokesman said pictures of the boat would be sent to scholars all over the country to determine from where the design of the boat originates.

"There may be a heritage of that type of boat somewhere else," Baker said. Or it could be a completely original design.

Kirk inherited the little boat when Teachout died alone in his shack over five years ago. The family that did exist for Teachout did not seem to care about his death, so Kirk made the arrangements for the funeral and his entire family attended. He didn't want Teachout to go out alone.

"He was a very, very gentle person," Kirk said.

The only thing Teachout left behind was his boat and Kirk refused to sell it even though he received many lucrative offers. So instead, it now sits in the Museum of Florida History, a memorial to a gentle Florida craftsman.

In Conclusion

When I arrived in 1989, as a newcomer I knew nothing of island history, flora, fauna, the Calusa Indians, or the Key Marco Cat. The 1895 Pepper Hearst Expedition with its 2,000 artifacts discovered in the muck of old Marco, was still a well-kept secret known only to some academics and a few local people. I also knew nothing of the early pioneers.

Bud Kirk is the one who should have written the book about Goodland and all the secret places he explored in the Everglades. That would have been the book to read.

For me the story of Goodland is Kappy Kirk's story, although Kappy died on October 16, 2010. We came to know one another pretty well despite the almost twenty year difference in our ages. Your friends are your friends no matter the age.

She was a proud third generation Florida Cracker and most generous about inviting me a "Newcomer" to meet her friends, family and neighbors, also first, second, and third generation Floridians.

Kappy was living alone in the house on Harbor Place when I met her, my memory of Kappy's house is that it was filled with people, sunlight, and roses - and a kitchen table that made everyone feel welcome.

Tributes
Marco Island Historical Museum Recognition
In Memory of Kappy Kirk, 2015

Katherine "Kappy" Kirk's name is prominently recognized on the Acknowledgement Panel among others who helped build the Pioneer Exhibit Gallery at the Marco Island Historical Museum.

Kappy Kirk Day, March 5, 2004

Kappy was recognized by the Marco Island City Council under leadership of Chairman Michael Minozzi proclaimed March 5, 2004 to be **Kappy Kirk Day** on her 87th Birthday. "In honor of her numerous and unselfish contributions to the citizens of Marco Island Whereas Volunteering of one's life has traditionally been and continues to be a part of the essence and tradition of our community, and Whereas, Whereas, Whereas (five in all) it is fitting to proclaim a special tribute to honor Mrs. Kirk for her dedication to making our community a better place to live."

www.ingramcontent.com/pod-product-compliance
Lightning Source LLC
Chambersburg PA
CBHW081458040426
42446CB00016B/3305